pans; let cool completely on wire racks. Yield: 4 dozen (serving size: 2 cookies).

Note: Store remaining cookies in an airtight container at room temperature up to 1 week, or freeze up to 1 month.

Points: 3; **Exchanges:** 1 Starch, 1 Fat
Per serving: CAL 126 (32% from fat); PRO 2.4g; FAT 4.4g (sat 0.8g); CARB 19.4g; FIB 0.8g; CHOL 0mg; IRON 1mg; SOD 134mg; CALC 24mg

---

LUNCH FOR TWO

Serves 2

Terrific Turkey Pockets

Greek Coleslaw

Terrific Turkey Pockets

4   ounces sliced cooked turkey breast
1   (8-inch) whole-wheat pita bread round, cut in half

2   tablespoons fat-free Italian dressing
2   (¾-ounce) slices fat-free cheddar processed cheese
¼   cup chopped tomato
½   cup alfalfa sprouts

1. Preheat oven to 400°.

2. Divide turkey between pita halves; spoon dressing over turkey. Place 1 cheese slice in each pita half. Wrap pitas in foil; bake at 400° for 5 minutes or until cheese melts. Top each pita half with tomato and alfalfa sprouts. Yield: 2 servings.

Points: 5; **Exchanges:** 3 Very Lean Meat, 2 Starch
Per serving: CAL 256 (10% from fat); PRO 26.5g; FAT 2.9g (sat 0.6g); CARB 27.4g; FIB 2.4g; CHOL 43mg; IRON 2.4mg; SOD 515mg; CALC 208mg

Greek Coleslaw

2   tablespoons fat-free sour cream
2   tablespoons red wine vinegar
½   teaspoon sugar
¼   teaspoon garlic powder
⅛   teaspoon salt

Broccoli-Cheese-Stuffed Potatoes are a meal in themselves.

Chickpeas provide ample protein in these meatless Mediterranean Pitas.

⅛ teaspoon pepper
1 cup shredded green cabbage
¼ cup shredded carrot
1 tablespoon chopped cucumber
1 tablespoon crumbled feta cheese
1½ teaspoons chopped green onions
1½ teaspoons chopped salad olives
1½ teaspoons sliced almonds, toasted

1. Combine first 6 ingredients in a bowl; stir with a whisk until blended.

2. Combine cabbage and next 6 ingredients in a bowl. Pour dressing over slaw; toss gently to coat. Yield: 2 servings.

Points: 1; **Exchanges:** ½ Starch, ½ Fat
Per serving: CAL 64 (28% from fat); PRO 2.9g; FAT 2g (sat 0.7g); CARB 9.1g; FIB 2.5g; CHOL 3mg; IRON 0.7mg; SOD 246mg; CALC 91mg

---

PICNIC IN THE PARK

Serves 8

Mediterranean Pitas

Carrot sticks and red bell pepper strips
(1 cup per person)

Mint-Cream Cheese Brownies

Mediterranean Pitas

Mediterranean Pitas are a natural for picnics. Make the bean mixture ahead, and add the toppings right before eating.

1 (19-ounce) can chickpeas (garbanzo beans), undrained
2 tablespoons sliced green onions
2 tablespoons sesame seeds, toasted
1½ tablespoons lemon juice
⅛ teaspoon salt
⅛ teaspoon hot sauce
1 garlic clove, minced
8 (8-inch) pita bread rounds
8 curly leaf lettuce leaves
2 cups alfalfa sprouts
1 medium cucumber, thinly sliced
½ cup plain fat-free yogurt

1. Drain beans, reserving 2 tablespoons liquid. Place beans, reserved liquid, green onions, and next 5 ingredients in a food processor; process until mixture is smooth, scraping sides of processor bowl once.

2. Spread bean mixture evenly over pita rounds. Place 1 lettuce leaf on each pita. Divide alfalfa sprouts and cucumber slices evenly among pitas. Drizzle fat-free yogurt evenly over cucumbers, and roll up pitas. Wrap bottom of each pita in wax paper or decorative paper. Serve immediately. Yield: 8 servings.

Points: 5; **Exchanges:** 3 Starch, 1 Veg, ½ Fat
Per serving: CAL 298 (11% from fat); PRO 9.6g; FAT 3.7g (sat 0.5g); CARB 53.5g; FIB 4.1g; CHOL 0mg; IRON 3.9mg; SOD 586mg; CALC 128mg

Mint-Cream Cheese Brownies

1 cup sugar
⅔ cup unsweetened cocoa
⅓ cup all-purpose flour
½ teaspoon baking powder
4 large egg whites, lightly beaten
¼ cup vegetable oil
1 teaspoon vanilla extract
¼ teaspoon peppermint extract
Cooking spray
6 ounces block fat-free cream cheese (about ¾ cup)
3 tablespoons sugar
1 tablespoon all-purpose flour

½ teaspoon vanilla extract
¼ teaspoon peppermint extract
1 large egg white

1. Preheat oven to 350°.

2. Combine first 4 ingredients in a large bowl; stir well. Combine 4 egg whites and next 3 ingredients in a small bowl; stir well. Add egg white mixture to dry ingredients, stirring well. Spread batter into an 8-inch square baking pan coated with cooking spray.

3. Combine cream cheese and next 5 ingredients in a medium bowl; beat at low speed of a mixer until mixture is smooth. Spoon cream cheese mixture by tablespoons over batter. Swirl cream cheese mixture and batter with a knife to create a marbled effect. Bake at 350° for 22 minutes or until a wooden pick inserted in center comes out almost clean. Let cool completely in pan on a wire rack. Cut into bars. Yield: 1 dozen (serving size: 1 brownie).

Note: Store remaining brownies in an airtight container at room temperature up to 1 week, or freeze up to 1 month.

Points: 4; **Exchanges:** 1½ Starch, 1 Fat
Per serving: CAL 174 (27% from fat); PRO 5.2g; FAT 5.2g (sat 1.2g); CARB 26g; FIB 0.1g; CHOL 3mg; IRON 1.1mg; SOD 109mg; CALC 60mg

CHASE AWAY THE CHILL MEAL

Serves 6

Winter Squash-and-White Bean Soup

Fruit salad

(1 cup assorted cut fruit with 1 tablespoon fat-free poppyseed dressing per person)

Almond Biscotti

Winter Squash-and-White Bean Soup

A bowlful of this soup counts as two of the five daily servings of fruits and vegetables recommended by the RDA.

1 tablespoon vegetable oil
1 cup finely chopped onion
¾ teaspoon ground cinnamon
½ teaspoon ground cumin
1 garlic clove, minced
3 cups (½-inch) cubed peeled butternut squash (about 1½ pounds)
⅛ teaspoon pepper
2 (10½-ounce) cans low-salt chicken broth
1 (14½-ounce) can Mexican-style stewed tomatoes, undrained
1 (14½-ounce) can no-salt-added whole tomatoes, undrained and chopped
1 (16-ounce) can cannellini beans, drained
6 tablespoons (1½ ounces) freshly grated Parmesan cheese

1. Heat oil in a large Dutch oven over medium heat. Add onion and next 3 ingredients; sauté 5 minutes or until onion is tender. Add squash and next 4 ingredients, and bring to a boil. Cover, reduce heat, and simmer 30 minutes or until squash is tender.

2. Place 2 cups of squash mixture in a blender, and process until smooth. Return squash purée to pan. Stir in beans, and cook over medium heat 5 minutes or until thoroughly heated. Ladle into

Puréed butternut squash adds creaminess to Winter Squash-and-White Bean Soup.

individual bowls, and sprinkle with Parmesan cheese. Yield: 6 servings (serving size: 1½ cups soup and 1 tablespoon cheese).

Points: 4; **Exchanges:** ½ Lean Meat, 1½ Starch, 1 Veg, ½ Fat
Per serving: CAL 196 (24% from fat); PRO 9.7g; FAT 5.3g (sat 1.9g); CARB 30.1g; FIB 3.4g; CHOL 5mg; IRON 3.2mg; SOD 455mg; CALC 186mg

Almond Biscotti

½   cup sugar
¼   cup stick margarine, softened
1   teaspoon almond extract
¼   teaspoon anise or vanilla extract
2   large eggs
1¾ cups all-purpose flour, divided
½   cup ground almonds
1   teaspoon baking powder
¼   teaspoon salt
Cooking spray

1. Combine first 5 ingredients in a bowl; beat at medium speed of a mixer until well blended. Combine 1½ cups flour, almonds, baking powder, and salt; stir well. Add almond mixture to egg mixture; beat well. Stir in remaining ¼ cup flour to make a soft dough. Cover; chill dough at least 2 hours.

Try dipping Almond Biscotti in coffee or dessert wine.

2. Preheat oven to 350°.

3. Turn dough out onto a lightly floured surface, and knead lightly 7 or 8 times. Divide dough in half; shape each half into a 12-inch-long log. Place logs on a baking sheet coated with cooking spray; flatten logs to a ¾-inch thickness. Bake at 350° for 20 minutes. Remove logs from pan; let cool 10 minutes on a wire rack. Reduce oven temperature to 300°.

4. Cut logs diagonally into ¼-inch slices. Place slices, cut sides down, on baking sheets. Bake at 300° for 15 minutes; turn cookies over, and bake an additional 15 minutes or until dry. Let cool on wire racks. Yield: 4 dozen (serving size: 2 cookies).

Note: Store remaining cookies in an airtight container at room temperature up to 1 week, or freeze up to 1 month.

Points: 2; **Exchanges:** ½ Starch, 1 Fat
Per serving: CAL 84 (39% from fat); PRO 2g; FAT 3.6g (sat 0.3g); CARB 11g; FIB 0.8g; CHOL 16mg; IRON 0.6mg; SOD 64mg; CALC 18mg

GARDEN CLUB LUNCHEON

Serves 4

Crabmeat Salad on English Muffins
Gazpacho

Crabmeat Salad on English Muffins

1   (2-ounce) jar diced pimiento, drained
¼   cup finely chopped celery
2   tablespoons chopped green onions
1½ tablespoons fat-free mayonnaise
1½ teaspoons prepared mustard
½   teaspoon lemon juice
1   cup lump crabmeat, shell pieces removed
2   English muffins, split and toasted
4   (¼-inch-thick) slices tomato
¼   cup (1 ounce) shredded reduced-fat sharp cheddar cheese
Freshly ground pepper

1. Combine first 6 ingredients in a medium bowl; stir well. Add crabmeat; toss gently. Place toasted English muffin halves on a baking sheet;

top each with crabmeat mixture, tomato slices, and cheese. Sprinkle with pepper. Broil 3 minutes or until cheese melts. Yield: 4 servings.

Points: 3; **Exchanges:** 1 Very Lean Meat, 1½ Starch
Per serving: CAL 164 (16% from fat); PRO 12.5g; FAT 2.9g (sat 1.4g); CARB 21.8g; FIB 0.7g; CHOL 40mg; IRON 1.8mg; SOD 425mg; CALC 163mg

Gazpacho

1½ cups no-salt-added tomato juice
3 large tomatoes, quartered and seeded
1 small cucumber, peeled, quartered, and seeded
1 small green bell pepper, quartered and seeded
1 small onion, peeled and quartered
1 garlic clove, peeled
2 tablespoons balsamic vinegar
½ teaspoon salt
¼ teaspoon hot sauce
¼ cup sliced cucumber
¼ cup finely chopped green bell pepper

1. Place first 6 ingredients in a food processor; process until smooth. Pour mixture into a large bowl; stir in vinegar, salt, and hot sauce. Cover and chill at least 2 hours. Ladle soup into bowls; top with cucumber slices and finely chopped bell pepper. Serve chilled. Yield: 4 servings (serving size: 1½ cups).

Points: 1; **Exchanges:** 3 Veg
Per serving: CAL 78 (10% from fat); PRO 3.3g; FAT 0.9g (sat 0g); CARB 17.7g; FIB 3.6g; CHOL 0mg; IRON 1.5mg; SOD 324mg; CALC 21mg

---

SATURDAY FARE

Serves 6

Sloppy Joes

Steak Fries

Sloppy Joes

2 pounds ground round
1½ cups chopped onion
½ cup chopped green bell pepper
2 garlic cloves, minced
⅔ cup water
½ cup no-salt-added ketchup

2 tablespoons prepared mustard
2 teaspoons chili powder
1½ teaspoons ground cumin
½ teaspoon salt
¼ teaspoon pepper
2 (8-ounce) cans no-salt-added tomato sauce
1 (15-ounce) can black beans, drained
1 (14-ounce) can no-salt-added whole tomatoes, drained and chopped
1 (6-ounce) can tomato paste
13 (1½-ounce) hamburger buns

1. Cook beef, onion, bell pepper, and garlic in a large Dutch oven over medium heat until browned, stirring to crumble beef. Drain mixture in a colander. Wipe drippings from pan with a paper towel.

2. Return beef mixture to pan. Add water and next 10 ingredients; stir well. Bring to a boil; cover, reduce heat, and simmer 30 minutes, stirring occasionally. Serve with hamburger buns. Yield: 13 servings (serving size: 1 bun and ⅔ cup meat mixture).

Points: 7; **Exchanges:** 2 Lean Meat, 2½ Starch
Per serving: CAL 320 (24% from fat); PRO 21.5g; FAT 8.4g (sat 2.1g); CARB 39.4g; FIB 2g; CHOL 57mg; IRON 3.7mg; SOD 347mg; CALC 52mg

Steak Fries

5 medium red potatoes (about 1¾ pounds)
1 tablespoon olive oil
¼ teaspoon salt
¼ teaspoon pepper
⅛ teaspoon ground nutmeg
1 garlic clove, crushed

1. Preheat oven to 450°.

2. Peel potatoes; cut each potato lengthwise into 6 wedges. Pat potato wedges dry with paper towels, and place in an 11- x 7-inch baking dish. Drizzle olive oil over potato wedges. Sprinkle with salt, pepper, nutmeg, and garlic; toss well. Bake potatoes at 450° for 30 minutes or until tender, stirring occasionally. Yield: 6 servings (serving size: 5 wedges).

Points: 2; **Exchanges:** 1 Starch, ½ Fat
Per serving: CAL 110 (20% from fat); PRO 2.4g; FAT 2.4g (sat 0.5g); CARB 20.5g; FIB 1.8g; CHOL 0mg; IRON 0.9mg; SOD 105mg; CALC 9mg

These slightly sweet Italian dessert biscuits get their intensely crunchy texture from twice-baking.

1 Kneading dough
Turn dough out onto a lightly floured surface (dough may be slightly dry). Knead dough lightly 7 or 8 times.

2 Rolling dough
Divide dough in half, and shape each half into a 12-inch-long log. Flatten logs to a ¾-inch thickness.

3 Cutting cookies
Let cool for 10 minutes; then slice the rolls diagonally. Bake the slices at 300° for 15 minutes on each side.

Remembrance Of Things Past

OUR LOW-FAT VERSIONS OF THESE AMERICAN CLASSICS ARE EVEN BETTER THAN THE DINER FAVORITES THAT INSPIRED THEM.

The origins of the phrase "blue plate special" are difficult to trace, but there's no denying the emotion and the place it conveys. Price-fixed meals that included meat loaf and mashed potatoes or pork chops and applesauce were once served on blue plates divided into small compartments. And while few of us ever actually ate off divided blue plates, we're all familiar with the institution that created this American idiom. Hear those words and you're transported to a joint with Naugahyde booths, linoleum countertops, and short-order cooks in white undershirts and matching paper caps. A place where the mayor, the mail carrier, and your geometry teacher sit side by side on swivel stools and the waitresses call everyone "hon" without offending anyone.

The recipes on the following pages can help you resurrect the past. Using low-fat cooking techniques and flavorful ingredients, we've improved crowd pleasers such as pot roast and baked apples and fried catfish and hush puppies. Unfortunately most of the quaint establishments that created these dishes have gone the way of the handwritten letter. But the makings of a blue plate special don't have to.

Garden-fresh parsley and basil enhance Crispy Herbed Chicken.

Simple flavors make Lemon-Dill Carrots a versatile side dish.

Combine buttermilk and lemon juice; brush over both sides of chicken breast halves. Add chicken to bag; seal bag, and shake to coat chicken.

3. Place chicken on a broiler pan coated with cooking spray. Sprinkle any remaining breadcrumb mixture over chicken. Bake, uncovered, at 400° for 40 minutes or until done. Garnish with lemon slices and parsley sprigs, if desired. Yield: 6 servings.

Points: 3; **Exchanges:** 4 Very Lean Meat, ½ Starch
Per serving: CAL 167 (11% from fat); PRO 29.5g; FAT 2g (sat 0.5g); CARB 6.5g; FIB 0.5g; CHOL 71mg; IRON 1.3mg; SOD 345mg; CALC 42mg

Lemon-Dill Carrots

8 medium carrots, diagonally sliced
1 teaspoon cornstarch
1 tablespoon lemon juice
⅓ cup water
1 teaspoon stick margarine
½ teaspoon dried dill
¼ teaspoon grated lemon rind
⅛ teaspoon salt
Dill sprigs (optional)

1. Steam carrot, covered, 3 minutes or until crisp-tender; drain. Set aside, and keep warm.

2. Combine cornstarch and lemon juice in a small saucepan; stir until well blended. Stir in water. Place over medium heat, and cook until thick, stirring constantly. Add margarine and next 3 ingredients; cook until margarine melts, stirring constantly. Pour sauce over carrots; toss gently. Garnish with dill sprigs, if desired. Yield: 6 servings (serving size: ⅔ cup).

Points: 0; **Exchanges:** 2 Veg
Per serving: CAL 55 (13% from fat); PRO 1.2g; FAT 0.8g (sat 0.1g); CARB 11.7g; FIB 3.5g; CHOL 0mg; IRON 0.5mg; SOD 95mg; CALC 32mg

Honeyed Banana Sauté

This dessert goes together in a moment's notice.

3 medium bananas, peeled and cut into ½-inch pieces
1 tablespoon lemon juice
2 teaspoons reduced-calorie stick margarine
1½ tablespoons honey
⅛ teaspoon grated lemon rind

SUNDAY SUPPER

Serves 6

Crispy Herbed Chicken

Lemon-Dill Carrots

Rice pilaf (½ cup per person)

Dinner rolls (1 per person)

Honeyed Banana Sauté

Crispy Herbed Chicken

This winning replacement for fried chicken is healthier and eliminates messy frying.

1¼ cups fresh whole-wheat breadcrumbs (about 2 slices)
1½ tablespoons minced fresh parsley
1 tablespoon chopped fresh basil
1½ teaspoons grated lemon rind
½ teaspoon salt
½ teaspoon pepper
3 tablespoons low-fat buttermilk
¾ teaspoon lemon juice
6 (6-ounce) skinned chicken breast halves
Cooking spray
Lemon slices (optional)
Parsley sprigs (optional)

1. Preheat oven to 400°.

2. Combine first 6 ingredients in a large heavy-duty, zip-top plastic bag. Seal bag, and shake well.

PREVENT

By day: A light but superbly effective moisturizer that's your skin's first line of defense against everyday sun and pollution. Use it alone or under makeup, but never be without it. SPF 15 for everyday, year-round protection. Enriched with vitamins which are natural anti-oxidants to boost skin's defenses.

POND'S®

AGE DEFYING SYSTEM

☀ PREVENT ☀

☾ CORRECT ☾

CORRECT

By night: A richer formulation, but still quickly and easily absorbed. Correct works while you sleep – delivering 3 alpha hydroxys and vitamins to help undo the signs of premature aging, smoothing, firming, encouraging newer skin cells to emerge, creating new radiance. Wake up. It's a new day for your skin.

QUICK&EASY
menus

Front cover: Spinach Lasagna, page 62; photography by Becky Luigart-Stayner, styling by Cathy Muir, and food styling by Jan A. Smith.

Editor: **Alyson Moreland Haynes**
Art Director: **Amy Heise**
Assistant Art Director: **Craig Hyde**
Managing Editor: **Kay Fuston**
Senior Writer: **Kate Neale Cooper**
Assistant Food Editor: **Regan Miller, R.D.**
Copy Editors: **Maria Parker Hopkins, Carol Boker**
Copy/Production Assistant: **Kate McWhorter**

Photographers: **Ralph Anderson, Jim Bathie, Tina Cornett,
Colleen Duffley, Becky Luigart-Stayner, Randy Mayor, Howard L. Puckett**
Photo Stylists: **Cindy Manning Barr, Kay E. Clarke, Melanie J. Clarke,
Virginia R. Cravens, Mary Catherine Muir, Fonda Shaia, Ashley J. Wyatt**
Food Stylist: **Iris Crawley O'Brien**

Weight Watchers Magazine Test Kitchens Director: **Kathleen Royal Phillips**
Assistant Director: **Gayle Hays Sadler** Staff: **Julie Christopher, Natalie E. King,
L. Victoria Knowles, Rebecca W. Mohr, Jan A. Smith, Kate M. Wheeler, R.D.**

Editor, *Weight Watchers* Magazine: **Kate Greer**
Executive Editor: **Mary Kay Culpepper**
Art Director: **Jamie Ezra Mark**
Assistant Editor: **Joe Watts**
Editorial Coordinator: **Christine O'Connell**

Senior Vice President, Publisher: **Jeffrey C. Ward**
General Manager: **Vicki A. Denmark**
Business Manager: **Michael W. Stern**
Marketing Manager: **Betsey Hummel**
Production Manager: **Robin Boteler**

President and CEO: **Tom Angelillo**
Executive Vice Presidents: **Bruce Akin, Jeanetta Keller, Scott Sheppard**
Vice President, Administration: **Lane Schmitt**
Vice President, Corporate Marketing: **Greg Keyes**
Vice President, Consumer Marketing: **Pat Vander Meer**
Vice President, Finance: **Bruce Larson**
Vice President, Production: **Larry Rinehart**

Back cover: Marbled Cheesecake, page 54;

photography by Howard L. Puckett, styling by Cindy Manning Barr.

WELCOME

Customs have the power to nurture, heal, and comfort us. Whether it's blowing out birthday candles, singing the national anthem before a baseball game, throwing rice at the bride and groom, or toasting the New Year, customs provide emotional reference points and a soothing expectation of what happens when. But even the most traditional among us realizes that the happiest of lives are those that gently sway between the comfort of the known and the energy of the new. A new job, a new home, a new love can put a sparkle in a life that's begun to yawn.

Nowhere is this life lesson more obvious than in our diets. The Thanksgiving turkey and Sunday brunch are wonderful culinary customs, but as anyone who has survived on a month of baked potatoes can attest, nothing gets older quicker than a culinary repeat performance. As children we find repetition reassuring, so we don't mind eating the same foods all the time; as adults it's usually because we've lost our imagination. Coming up with new recipe ideas is especially hard when you're watching your weight. Too often, the same exact food at precisely the right time becomes a way to calm and eliminate our sense of being out of control.

It is a noble and normal response, but it is just a starting point. A healthy lifestyle is one that embraces variety. Diets that include a wide number of foods not only increase the body's ability to reap nutritional benefits but also may help prevent disease. In addition, studies suggest that getting in a food rut can set you up for binges and long-term diet failure.

Quick & Easy Menus expands your cooking—and eating—horizons without confining you to the kitchen. This cookbook includes more than 130 low-fat recipes for everything from a make-ahead Greek Shrimp Salad for your next potluck dinner to Pesto Lamb Chops for the Friday night your mom has agreed to keep the kids. Each recipe and menu in this cookbook includes POINTS, the basis for following the Weight Watchers 1•2•3 Success™ Weight Loss Plan. We've also counted all the calories—along with protein, fat, carbohydrates, fiber, cholesterol, iron, sodium, and calcium—and included diabetic exchanges for people with special dietary restrictions.

And because planning meals is often more work than cooking them, we've rounded out our recipes and provided 52 complete menus. Whether the meal is for a celebration (Special Occasions) or an everyday evening (Blue Plate Specials), you won't have to rely on the food muses for inspiration anymore.

Alyson M. Haynes

QUICK&EASY
menus

c o n t e n t s

Sunny Side Up

START OFF ON THE RIGHT NUTRITIONAL FOOT
AND YOU'LL EAT MORE HEALTHFULLY
ALL DAY LONG.

*B*reakfast *is your first chance to start the day right. Most importantly, eating breakfast is a sound nutritional practice. One study showed that women who ate three meals a day lost more weight than those who skipped breakfast. For those trained in the old "diet equals starvation" school of weight loss this seems illogical, but nutritionists say it makes perfect sense. Here's why: Eating breakfast increases your body's metabolic rate, which means you burn more calories all day. Skip this meal and it's harder to resist the urge to snack.*

But it's not just about nourishment. There's no greater luxury than breakfast in bed or a celebratory champagne brunch. So this chapter includes recipes such as Ham-and-Cheese Strata for leisurely weekends, as well as portable breakfasts such as Apple-and-Spice Muffins for the weekday rush. And just because it's the day's most important meal doesn't mean it should consume your morning. Some of these recipes incorporate shortcuts (the Dill Rolls don't require kneading) and others, such as the Oatmeal-Date Bars, can be made ahead and enjoyed throughout the week.

Serve Oatmeal-Date Bars for breakfast or as a healthy snack.

Breakfast Pita Sandwiches

Cooking spray
1   cup thinly sliced mushrooms
½   cup chopped onion
½   cup finely chopped red bell pepper
2   cups egg substitute
½   cup 1% low-fat cottage cheese
¼   teaspoon pepper
½   cup (2 ounces) shredded reduced-fat cheddar cheese
2   (6-inch) whole-wheat pita bread rounds, cut in half

1. Coat a medium nonstick skillet with cooking spray; place over medium-high heat until hot. Add mushrooms, onion, and bell pepper; sauté 4 minutes or until tender.

2. Combine egg substitute, cottage cheese, and pepper in a small bowl; stir well. Pour over vegetables, and cook over medium heat until mixture is firm but still moist, stirring frequently. Add cheddar cheese, stirring just until cheese melts. Spoon mixture evenly into whole-wheat pita halves. Serve sandwiches immediately. Yield: 4 servings.

Points: 5; **Exchanges:** 2 Lean Meat, 1 Veg, 1½ Starch
Per serving: CAL 256 (15% from fat); PRO 22.5g; FAT 4.2g (sat 1.8g); CARB 28.6g; FIB 1.4g; CHOL 10mg; IRON 3.9mg; SOD 508mg; CALC 400mg

Oatmeal-Date Bars

1½ cups chopped dates
¾   cup water
2½ tablespoons lemon juice
⅓   cup stick margarine, softened
⅔   cup firmly packed brown sugar
1   teaspoon vanilla extract
1   cup regular oats
¾   cup all-purpose flour
¼   cup whole-wheat flour

½   teaspoon baking soda
⅛   teaspoon salt
Cooking spray

1. Preheat oven to 375°.

2. Combine dates, water, and lemon juice in a medium saucepan; bring to a boil. Reduce heat, and simmer, uncovered, 5 minutes or until thick, stirring frequently. Remove from heat; set aside.

3. Cream margarine. Gradually add brown sugar, beating at medium speed of a mixer until light and fluffy. Add vanilla; beat well. Combine oats and next 4 ingredients; stir well. Add oat mixture to creamed mixture, stirring until mixture resembles coarse meal.

4. Press 2 cups oat mixture evenly into a 9-inch square baking pan coated with cooking spray; set remaining oat mixture aside. Bake at 375° for 5 minutes or until crust is puffy.

5. Spread date mixture over prepared crust, and sprinkle with remaining oat mixture. Bake at 375° for 20 minutes or until golden. Let cool in pan on a wire rack. Cut into bars. Yield: 16 bars (serving size: 1 bar).

Note: Store remaining bars in an airtight container at room temperature up to 5 days.

Points: 3; **Exchanges:** 1 Fruit, 1 Starch, ½ Fat
Per serving: CAL 159 (24% from fat); PRO 2g; FAT 4.3g (sat 0.8g); CARB 29.7g; FIB 2.3g; CHOL 0mg; IRON 0.9mg; SOD 92mg; CALC 19mg

Strawberry-Orange Shake

2   cups unsweetened frozen strawberries
1   cup chilled orange juice
1   cup skim milk
1   (8-ounce) carton strawberry low-fat yogurt

1. Place frozen strawberries, orange juice, and skim milk in a blender; process just until blended. Add yogurt; process just until blended. Pour into chilled glasses; serve immediately. Yield: 4 servings (serving size: 1¼ cups).

Points: 3; **Exchanges:** 1 Fruit, 1 Sk Milk
Per serving: CAL 145 (6% from fat); PRO 5.2g; FAT 0.9g (sat 0.5g); CARB 30.6g; FIB 1.1g; CHOL 3mg; IRON 1mg; SOD 65mg; CALC 177mg

Strawberry-Orange Shake

Granola Pancakes

Skim milk is all you need to round out this breakfast rich in grains and fruit.

⅓ cup all-purpose flour
¼ cup whole-wheat flour
1 teaspoon baking powder
Dash of salt
2 teaspoons sugar
¼ teaspoon ground cinnamon
⅓ cup skim milk
¼ cup low-fat granola without raisins, crushed
1½ teaspoons vegetable oil
1 large egg white, lightly beaten
Cooking spray
¼ cup maple syrup

1. Combine first 6 ingredients in a medium bowl; make a well in center of mixture. Combine milk, granola, oil, and egg white; add to dry ingredients, stirring just until moist.

2. Spoon about ¼ cup batter for each pancake onto a hot nonstick griddle or skillet coated with cooking spray, spreading batter to a 4-inch circle. Turn pancakes when tops are covered with bubbles and edges look cooked. Serve with syrup. Yield: 4 (4-inch) pancakes (serving size: 2 pancakes and 2 tablespoons syrup).

Points: 7; **Exchanges:** 4½ Starch
Per serving: CAL 344 (13% from fat); PRO 8.2g; FAT 5.1g (sat 0.9g); CARB 68.5g; FIB 3.2g; CHOL 1mg; IRON 2.7mg; SOD 224mg; CALC 181mg

Fruit Kabobs

1 small banana, cut into 1-inch chunks
1 tablespoon pineapple juice
8 canned unsweetened pineapple chunks, drained
½ kiwifruit, cut into 4 wedges
4 large strawberries

1. Combine banana chunks and pineapple juice in a bowl, and toss gently; drain. Thread fruit alternately onto 4 small wooden skewers. Serve kabobs immediately. Yield: 2 servings (serving size: 2 kabobs).

Points: 1; **Exchanges:** 1½ Fruit
Per serving: CAL 89 (4% from fat); PRO 0.9g; FAT 0.4g (sat 0.1g); CARB 21.7g; FIB 2.8g; CHOL 0mg; IRON 0.5mg; SOD 1mg; CALC 17mg

---

SATURDAY MORNING SPECIAL

Serves 4

Raisin Bread French Toast
With Apple Syrup

Spicy Pork Sausage

Brown Sugar-Pecan Baked Citrus

Raisin Bread French Toast With Apple Syrup

¼ cup apple cider
2 tablespoons low-sugar apple jelly
1 tablespoon brown sugar
½ teaspoon cornstarch
⅔ cup egg substitute
¼ cup skim milk
½ teaspoon vanilla extract
Cooking spray
4 (1-ounce) slices cinnamon-raisin bread

1. Combine first 4 ingredients in a small saucepan, and stir well. Place over medium heat, and cook until jelly melts and mixture is slightly thick, stirring constantly. Remove from heat; set aside, and keep warm.

2. Combine egg substitute, milk, and vanilla in a shallow dish; stir well. Coat a 10-inch cast-iron skillet with cooking spray; place over medium heat until hot. Dip 2 bread slices in egg mixture, coating both sides of bread. Place bread in skillet; cook 3 minutes on each side or until browned. Repeat with remaining bread and egg mixture. Serve warm with cider mixture. Yield: 4 servings.

Points: 3; **Exchanges:** 1½ Starch, ½ Very Lean Meat
Per serving: CAL 134 (7% from fat); PRO 6.2g; FAT 1g (sat 0.2g); CARB 24.7g; FIB 1.1g; CHOL 1mg; IRON 1.1mg; SOD 177mg; CALC 55mg

Spicy Pork Sausage

If prepackaged lean ground pork is not available at your grocery store, ask the butcher to grind some lean pork loin for you.

6 ounces lean ground pork
1½ tablespoons dry breadcrumbs
1 tablespoon finely chopped onion
½ teaspoon rubbed sage
¼ teaspoon fennel seeds, crushed
¼ teaspoon ground thyme
¼ teaspoon hot sauce
⅛ teaspoon salt
⅛ teaspoon garlic powder
⅛ teaspoon ground red pepper
⅛ teaspoon pepper
1 large egg white, lightly beaten
Cooking spray

1. Combine first 12 ingredients in a bowl; stir well. Shape mixture into 8 links.

2. Coat a large cast-iron skillet with cooking spray, and place over medium heat until hot. Place sausage links in skillet, and cook 10 minutes or until browned, turning frequently. Drain links on paper towels. Serve warm. Yield: 8 links (serving size: 2 links).

Points: 2; **Exchanges:** 1 Med-fat Meat
Per serving: CAL 72 (38% from fat); PRO 9g; FAT 3g (sat 1g); CARB 2g; FIB 0.2g; CHOL 22mg; IRON 0.6mg; SOD 126mg; CALC 12mg

Brown Sugar-Pecan Baked Citrus

1 cup grapefruit sections
1 cup orange sections
1 tablespoon water
2½ teaspoons brown sugar
2 teaspoons reduced-calorie stick margarine, melted
2 teaspoons chopped pecans, toasted

1. Preheat oven to 400°.

2. Arrange grapefruit and orange sections in a baking dish. Combine water, sugar, and margarine; brush over fruit. Sprinkle with pecans. Bake at 400° for 8 minutes or until warm. Serve warm. Yield: 4 servings (serving size: ½ cup).

Points: 1; **Exchanges:** 1 Fruit, ½ Fat
Per serving: CAL 67 (30% from fat); PRO 0.9g; FAT 2.2g (sat 0.2g); CARB 12.5g; FIB 2.6g; CHOL 0mg; IRON 0.2mg; SOD 19mg; CALC 29mg

Brown Sugar-Pecan
Baked Citrus

Guests will appreciate an elegant brunch of Crabmeat Crepes, melon balls, and Lemon-Blueberry Muffins.

B R U N C H   O N   T H E   V E R A N D A

Serves 8

Crabmeat Crepes

Melon balls
(1 cup assorted melon balls per person)

Lemon-Blueberry Muffins

Mint Lover's Tea

Crabmeat Crepes

2   teaspoons reduced-calorie stick margarine
Cooking spray
1⅓ cups sliced mushrooms
1   cup chopped green onions
1   teaspoon dried whole thyme
1   tablespoon all-purpose flour
1   cup skim milk
1   pound lump crabmeat, shell pieces removed
2   tablespoons chopped fresh parsley
2   teaspoons lemon juice
¼   teaspoon salt
¼   teaspoon dry mustard
⅛   teaspoon ground red pepper
Light Crepes
Thyme sprigs (optional)

1. Melt margarine in a large nonstick skillet coated with cooking spray over medium-high heat. Add mushrooms, green onions, and dried thyme; sauté 3 minutes or until tender. Reduce heat to low; stir in flour. Cook 1 minute, stirring constantly. Gradually add milk, stirring constantly. Cook over medium heat until thick and bubbly, stirring constantly. Remove from heat; stir in crabmeat and next 5 ingredients.

2. Preheat oven to 350°.

3. Spoon 3 tablespoons crabmeat mixture down center of each Light Crepe; roll up crepes, and place, seam side down, in 2 (13- x 9-inch) baking dishes coated with cooking spray. Cover and bake at 350° for 15 minutes or until thoroughly heated. Uncover; broil crepes 1 minute or until golden. Garnish with thyme sprigs, if desired. Yield: 8 servings (serving size: 2 crepes).

LIGHT CREPES:
²⁄₃ cup all-purpose flour
1⅓ cups skim milk
4 large egg whites, lightly beaten
Cooking spray

1. Place flour in a medium bowl. Gradually add milk and egg whites, stirring with a whisk until smooth. Cover and chill batter at least 1 hour (this allows flour particles to swell and soften so the crepes are light in texture).

2. Coat a 6-inch nonstick crepe pan or skillet with cooking spray. Place over medium heat until hot. Remove pan from heat. Pour 2 tablespoons batter into pan, and quickly tilt pan in all directions so batter covers bottom of pan with a thin film. Cook approximately 1 minute. Carefully lift edge of crepe with a spatula to test for doneness. Crepe is ready to turn when it can be shaken loose from pan and underside is lightly browned. Turn crepe over, and cook 30 seconds (this side is usually spotty brown and is the side on which filling is placed).

3. Place crepe on a towel, and allow it to cool. Repeat procedure until all batter is used. Stack crepes between single layers of wax paper or paper towels to prevent them from sticking. Yield: 16 (6-inch) crepes.

Points: 3; Exchanges: 2 Very Lean Meat, 1 Starch
Per serving: CAL 144 (16% from fat); PRO 17.1g; FAT 2.5g (sat 0.4g); CARB 12.6g; FIB 0.7g; CHOL 58mg; IRON 1.6mg; SOD 307mg; CALC 161mg

Lemon-Blueberry Muffins

2 tablespoons sugar
1 tablespoon lemon juice
2½ cups all-purpose flour
¼ cup sugar
2 teaspoons baking powder
½ teaspoon baking soda
¼ teaspoon salt
1½ cups low-fat buttermilk
¼ cup vegetable oil
¼ cup egg substitute
1 tablespoon grated lemon rind
1 teaspoon vanilla extract
1½ cups frozen blueberries, thawed
Cooking spray

1. Preheat oven to 375°.

2. Combine 2 tablespoons sugar and lemon juice; stir well, and set aside. Combine flour and next 4 ingredients in a large bowl, and make a well in center of mixture. Combine buttermilk and next 4 ingredients; add buttermilk mixture to dry ingredients, stirring just until moist. Gently fold in blueberries.

3. Divide batter evenly among large (2¼-inch) muffin cups coated with cooking spray. Bake at 375° for 20 minutes. Brush lemon juice mixture over muffins, and bake an additional 6 minutes or until muffins are golden. Remove from pans immediately. Let cool on wire racks. Yield: 1 dozen (serving size: 1 muffin).

Note: Store remaining muffins in an airtight container at room temperature up to 2 days, or freeze up to 1 month.

Points: 4; Exchanges: 1 Fat, 2 Starch
Per serving: CAL 192 (27% from fat); PRO 4.4g; FAT 5.8g (sat 1g); CARB 30.7g; FIB 1.4g; CHOL 1mg; IRON 1.4mg; SOD 126mg; CALC 91mg

Mint Lover's Tea

8 cups boiling water
1½ cups fresh mint leaves, chopped
3 tablespoons loose gunpowder tea
5 regular-size mint-herb tea bags
⅓ cup lime juice
⅓ cup honey
Mint sprigs, lemon or lime slices
    (optional)

1. Combine boiling water, chopped mint, loose tea, and tea bags in a pitcher; cover and steep 10 minutes. Strain mixture through a sieve into another pitcher; discard mint, loose tea, and tea bags. Add lime juice and honey to tea, and stir

Ideal for entertaining, crepes can be cooled, stacked in wax paper, and frozen in a zip-top bag up to 3 months.

Step One
Add milk and egg whites to flour; stir with a whisk until smooth. Chill 1 hour or overnight.

Step Two
Fill a ¼-cup measure half full with batter; pour batter into pan in a steady stream. Tilt to coat bottom of pan.

Step Three
Lift edge of crepe to check for doneness. Crepe should be light brown and easy to shake loose from pan.

Apple-and-Spice Muffins

1   cup all-purpose flour
1   cup whole-wheat flour
⅓   cup toasted wheat germ
¼   cup firmly packed brown sugar
1½ teaspoons baking powder
1   teaspoon ground cinnamon
½   teaspoon baking soda
¼   teaspoon salt
¼   teaspoon ground nutmeg
2   cups peeled shredded cooking apple
½   cup skim milk
2   tablespoons vegetable oil
1   teaspoon grated lemon rind
1   large egg, lightly beaten
2   large egg whites, lightly beaten
Cooking spray

1. Preheat oven to 400°.

2. Combine first 9 ingredients in a large bowl; make a well in center of mixture. Combine apple and next 5 ingredients; stir well, and add to dry ingredients, stirring just until moist.

3. Divide batter evenly among muffin cups coated with cooking spray. Bake at 400° for 10 minutes or until lightly browned. Remove muffins from pans immediately. Yield: 16 muffins (serving size: 2 muffins).

Points: 4; **Exchanges:** 2½ Starch, ½ Fat
Per serving: CAL 222 (23% from fat); PRO 7g; FAT 5.6g (sat 1.2g); CARB 37.4g; FIB 3.8g; CHOL 28mg; IRON 1mg; SOD 214mg; CALC 38mg

Citrus Spritzer

3   (3- x ½-inch) strips orange rind
3   (3- x ½-inch) strips grapefruit rind
4   cups pineapple-orange juice
2   cups fresh pink grapefruit juice
2   cups chilled sparkling mineral water

1. Place citrus strips in a glass pitcher; crush slightly by gently pressing against pitcher with back of a spoon. Add juices, and stir well. Cover and chill thoroughly. Stir in mineral water just before serving. Serve over ice. Yield: 2 quarts (serving size: 1 cup).

Points: 2; **Exchanges:** 1½ Fruit
Per serving: CAL 91 (2% from fat); PRO 0.6g; FAT 0.2g (sat 0g); CARB 22.4g; FIB 0g; CHOL 0mg; IRON 1.5mg; SOD 13mg; CALC 11mg

---

Gunpowder tea, lime juice, and honey give Mint Lover's Tea its unique flavor.

mixture well. Cover and chill. Serve tea over ice cubes. Garnish, if desired. Yield: 8 cups (serving size: 1 cup).

Note: To make Mint Ice Cubes, combine 4 cups boiling water and 2 cups crushed fresh mint leaves. Let cool completely, and discard mint leaves. Pour liquid into ice cube trays, and freeze until firm.

Points: 1; **Exchanges:** ½ Starch
Per serving: CAL 45 (0% from fat); PRO 0.1g; FAT 0g (sat 0g); CARB 12.5g; FIB 0g; CHOL 0mg; IRON 0.1mg; SOD 8mg; CALC 2mg

BUSY WEEKDAY BREAKFAST

Serves 8

Apple-and-Spice Muffins

Turkey bacon
(2 slices per person)

Citrus Spritzer

CELEBRATION BRUNCH

Serves 10

Ham-and-Cheese Strata

Steamed asparagus
(4 ounces per person)

Apple-Currant Biscuits

Almond Fruit Medley

Ham-and-Cheese Strata

Cooking spray
4 cups sliced mushrooms
¾ cup chopped green onions
½ cup chopped red bell pepper
1 (16-ounce) loaf French bread, torn into bite-size pieces
⅔ cup dry white wine
1¼ cups chopped lean, lower salt ham
1 cup (4 ounces) shredded reduced-fat Swiss cheese
1½ cups egg substitute
1½ cups skim milk
½ teaspoon dried thyme
½ teaspoon dry mustard
¼ teaspoon pepper
⅛ teaspoon salt

1. Coat a large nonstick skillet with cooking spray; place over medium-high heat until hot. Add mushrooms, green onions, and bell pepper; sauté until tender.

2. Coat a 13- x 9-inch baking dish with cooking spray. Place bread in dish; spoon mushroom mixture over bread. Pour wine over mushroom mixture; sprinkle with ham and cheese. Combine egg substitute and next 5 ingredients in a bowl; stir with a whisk until blended. Pour over cheese. Cover and chill 8 hours.

3. Preheat oven to 325°.

4. Let strata stand at room temperature 20 minutes before baking. Bake, covered, at 325° for 1 hour or until set. Yield: 10 servings.

Points: 5; **Exchanges:** 1½ Lean Meat, 2 Starch
Per serving: CAL 237 (16% from fat); PRO 17.4g; FAT 4.3g (sat 2g); CARB 31.1g; FIB 1.8g; CHOL 19mg; IRON 2.5mg; SOD 543mg; CALC 221mg

Apple-Currant Biscuits

⅓ cup dried currants
¼ cup apple juice
1¾ cups all-purpose flour
2 tablespoons sugar
2 teaspoons baking powder
1¼ teaspoons ground cinnamon
⅛ teaspoon salt
½ cup low-fat buttermilk
3 tablespoons margarine, melted
1 tablespoon all-purpose flour
Cooking spray
½ cup sifted powdered sugar
2 tablespoons apple juice

1. Combine currants and ¼ cup apple juice in a small bowl; let stand for 10 minutes. Drain, reserving juice and currants.

2. Preheat oven to 400°.

3. Combine 1¾ cups flour and next 4 ingredients in a medium bowl; make a well in center of mixture. Combine reserved juice, buttermilk, and margarine; add to dry ingredients, stirring just until moist. Stir in reserved currants.

4. Sprinkle 1 tablespoon flour evenly over work surface. Turn dough out onto floured surface; knead 4 or 5 times. Roll dough to a ½-inch thickness; cut with a 1½-inch biscuit cutter. Place on a baking sheet coated with cooking spray. Bake at 400° for 10 minutes or until golden.

5. Combine powdered sugar and 2 tablespoons juice; stir well. Drizzle over warm biscuits. Serve warm. Yield: 26 biscuits (serving size: 2 biscuits).

Note: Store remaining biscuits in an airtight container at room temperature up to 2 days, or freeze up to 1 month.

Points: 5; **Exchanges:** 1½ Starch, ½ Fat
Per serving: CAL 130 (21% from fat); PRO 2.4g; FAT 3g (sat 0.6g); CARB 23.8g; FIB 0.6g; CHOL 0mg; IRON 1mg; SOD 66mg; CALC 64mg

Almond Fruit Medley

⅓ cup sliced almonds
3 tablespoons sugar
6 nectarines, sliced
2 navel oranges, peeled and sectioned
2 plums, sliced
¼ cup orange juice

Discovered in China more than 5,000 years ago, and second only to water in international consumption, tea is the world's most popular beverage. Americans, who consume far less tea than the British and residents of the Far East, still manage to drink more than 50 billion cups or glasses of tea a year—that's more than 10 gallons per person.

•Iced tea, an American creation, was invented in 1904 at the World's Fair in St. Louis.

•Almost 85% of the tea consumed in the U.S. is served over ice.

•A cup of tea, depending on how it's brewed, has less than half the caffeine of a cup of coffee. It also contains no calories, no sodium, and, unless you add it, no sugar.

•Herbal teas aren't really teas at all but blends of natural grains, fruit flavors, spices, and plant parts such as flowers, leaves, and roots. Herbal tea is naturally caffeine-free.

1. Combine almonds and sugar in a nonstick skillet. Place over low heat, and cook 20 minutes or until sugar melts and coats almonds. Stir constantly. Spoon mixture onto a baking sheet; let cool. Break almond mixture into small chunks.

2. Combine fruit and orange juice in a large bowl; toss gently. Cover and chill. Divide fruit mixture evenly between compotes; top evenly with almond mixture. Yield: 10 servings.

Points: 2; **Exchanges:** 1½ Fruit, ½ Fat
Per serving: CAL 117 (12% from fat); PRO 1.6g; FAT 1.6g (sat 0.2g); CARB 23.3g; FIB 4.1g; CHOL 0mg; IRON 0.3mg; SOD 0mg; CALC 24mg

GRAB-'N'-GO

Serves 4

Breakfast on a Bagel

Orange Juicy

Breakfast on a Bagel

2   (2¼-ounce) plain bagels, split and toasted
4   (1-ounce) slices lean Canadian bacon
4   (½-inch) slices tomato
½   cup (2 ounces) shredded reduced-fat cheddar cheese

1. Place bagel halves, cut side up, on a baking sheet; top each with Canadian bacon, tomato, and cheese. Broil 2 minutes or until cheese melts. Yield: 4 servings.

Points: 4; **Exchanges:** 1½ Lean Meat, 1 Starch
Per serving: CAL 179 (27% from fat); PRO 13.6g; FAT 5.2g (sat 2.3g); CARB 18.8g; FIB 0.9g; CHOL 23mg; IRON 1mg; SOD 679mg; CALC 71mg

Orange Juicy

1   (6-ounce) can thawed orange juice concentrate, undiluted
1   cup water
1   cup skim milk
¼   cup sugar
1   teaspoon vanilla extract
Ice cubes

1. Combine first 5 ingredients in a blender; process until smooth. Add enough ice cubes to blender to bring mixture to 6-cup level, and process until smooth. Serve immediately. Yield: 4 servings (serving size: 1½ cups).

Points: 3; **Exchanges:** 1 Starch, 1 Fruit
Per serving: CAL 140 (1% from fat); PRO 3g; FAT 0.2g (sat 0.1g); CARB 32g; FIB 0g; CHOL 2mg; IRON 0.1mg; SOD 34mg; CALC 88mg

FARMER'S MARKET BRUNCH

Serves 6

Vegetable Omelets

Dill Rolls

Berries With Creamy Peach Topping

Vegetable Omelets

3   small red potatoes
Cooking spray
1½ teaspoons vegetable oil
1   cup sliced mushrooms
¾   cup chopped broccoli
½   cup chopped onion
½   cup chopped red bell pepper
1   teaspoon dried basil
¼   teaspoon freshly ground pepper
1   cup egg substitute
2   tablespoons orange juice
2   large egg whites
1   tablespoon all-purpose flour
¾   cup (3 ounces) shredded reduced-fat sharp cheddar cheese, divided
Basil sprigs (optional)

1. Place potatoes in a saucepan, and cover with water; bring to a boil. Cook 15 minutes or just until tender. Drain; let cool. Cut into thin slices.

2. Coat a nonstick skillet with cooking spray. Add oil; place over medium-high heat until hot. Add mushrooms and next 3 ingredients; sauté 6 minutes. Add potatoes, basil, and pepper; cook 1 minute. Remove from skillet. Set aside; keep warm.

3. Combine egg substitute and orange juice in a medium bowl; beat at medium speed of a mixer until foamy. Beat egg whites at high speed of a mixer until soft peaks form. Add flour; beat until stiff peaks form. Gently fold egg white mixture into egg substitute mixture. Recoat skillet with cooking spray; place over medium heat until hot.

Add one-third of egg mixture to skillet; spread evenly. Cover and cook 4 minutes or until set.

4. Spoon one-third of vegetable mixture over half of omelet. Sprinkle with ¼ cup cheese. Loosen omelet with a spatula; carefully fold in half. Slide omelet onto a serving platter; set aside, and keep warm. Repeat procedure twice with remaining egg mixture, vegetable mixture, and cheese. Cut each omelet in half just before serving. Garnish with basil sprigs, if desired. Serve warm. Yield: 6 servings (serving size: ½ omelet).

Points: 3; **Exchanges:** 1 Lean Meat, ½ Starch, 1 Veg
Per serving: CAL 125 (30% from fat); PRO 10.9g; FAT 4.2g (sat 1.8g); CARB 11.2g; FIB 1.5g; CHOL 9mg; IRON 1.7mg; SOD 186mg; CALC 153mg

Dill Rolls

This no-fuss bread doesn't require kneading.

1½ cups skim milk
⅓ cup stick margarine
3¾ cups all-purpose flour, divided
¼ cup sugar
2 teaspoons dried dill
½ teaspoon salt
1 package active dry yeast
¼ cup egg substitute
Cooking spray

1. Combine milk and margarine in a saucepan. Place over medium heat; cook until margarine melts, stirring occasionally. Remove from heat; let cool to 120° to 130°. Combine 1½ cups flour and next 4 ingredients. Gradually add milk mixture to flour mixture, beating at low speed of a mixer until blended. Add egg substitute; beat well. Gradually stir in enough of remaining 2¼ cups flour to make a soft dough (dough will be sticky).

2. Cover and let rise in warm place (85°), free from drafts, 45 minutes or until doubled in bulk. Stir dough down to remove air bubbles. Divide evenly among muffin cups coated with cooking spray. Cover; let rise 30 minutes or until doubled in bulk.

3. Preheat oven to 400°.

4. Bake at 400° for 15 minutes or until golden. Remove rolls from pans immediately, and serve warm. Yield: 1½ dozen (serving size: 1 roll).

Note: Store remaining rolls in an airtight container at room temperature up to 2 days, or freeze up to 1 month.

Points: 3; **Exchanges:** 1½ Starch, ½ Fat
Per serving: CAL 146 (23% from fat); PRO 3.9g; FAT 3.7g (sat 0.7g); CARB 23.9g; FIB 0.8g; CHOL 0mg; IRON 1.4mg; SOD 121mg; CALC 34mg

Berries With Creamy Peach Topping

1 cup frozen sliced peaches, thawed
¼ cup low-fat sour cream
1 tablespoon brown sugar
½ teaspoon lemon juice
3 cups fresh strawberry halves
1 cup fresh or frozen blackberries
Mint sprigs (optional)

1. Combine first 4 ingredients in a blender; process until smooth.

2. Divide berries evenly among dessert dishes; top evenly with peach mixture. Garnish with mint sprigs, if desired. Yield: 6 servings.

Points: 1; **Exchanges:** 1 Fruit
Per serving: CAL 64 (23% from fat); PRO 1.1g; FAT 1.6g (sat 0.8g); CARB 12.9g; FIB 4.3g; CHOL 4mg; IRON 0.5mg; SOD 5mg; CALC 32mg

Start your day with the garden-fresh flavors of Vegetable Omelets.

Let There Be Lunch

JUST BECAUSE IT'S SANDWICHED
BETWEEN BREAKFAST AND DINNER DOESN'T
MEAN THIS MEAL CAN'T BE EXCITING.

You can tell much about a person by peeking into her brown bag. Better than an outstretched palm, a lost Day-Timer, or even an unlocked diary, lunches reveal a host of personal details (especially at work). The neatnik prefers a host of compartmentalized containers. The family person brings a serving from last night's feast. And then you have your single folks, who tote a hodgepodge of items that meet two criteria: available and edible.

Granted, we should stay away from stereotypes, but the reason lunches are so revealing about a person's life and personality is that nothing is as predictable as lunch. So send the message that you're more than your turkey on wheat by livening up your noon repast. Just because it's the middle child of meals doesn't mean it should be relegated to happenstance. To keep you off a rut-ridden path, we've included a range of choices: Broccoli-Cheese-Stuffed Potatoes is a great option for a leisurely lunch at home, the Crabmeat Salad on English Muffins is perfect for midday entertaining, and the Mediterranean Pitas will make your colleagues think you have a Greece vacation in the works.

Cumin and orange give a subtle flavor twist to Vegetable-Couscous Salad.

Vegetable-Couscous Salad

1   cup plus 2 tablespoons water
¾   cup uncooked couscous
6   ounces fresh asparagus
½   cup diced yellow bell pepper
½   cup cherry tomatoes, quartered and seeded
¼   cup thinly sliced green onions
1½ tablespoons fat-free chicken broth
1   tablespoon thawed orange juice concentrate
1   tablespoon balsamic vinegar
1   teaspoon grated orange rind
1½ teaspoons olive oil
½   teaspoon ground cumin
¼   teaspoon salt
4   lettuce leaves (optional)

1. Bring water to a boil in a medium saucepan. Remove from heat. Stir in couscous; cover and let stand 5 minutes or until tender and liquid is absorbed. Fluff with a fork; set aside.

2. Snap off tough ends of asparagus; remove scales with a knife or vegetable peeler, if desired. Cut asparagus into 1-inch pieces. Cook in boiling water 1 minute or until crisp-tender. Drain and rinse under cold water, and drain again.

3. Combine asparagus, couscous, bell pepper, tomatoes, and onions; toss gently. Combine broth and next 6 ingredients; stir well with a whisk. Pour over salad; toss gently to coat. Cover; chill at least 8 hours. Serve on lettuce-lined salad plates, if desired. Yield: 4 servings (serving size: 1 cup).

Points: 3; **Exchanges:** 2 Starch
Per serving: CAL 174 (10% from fat); PRO 6.1g; FAT 2g (sat 0.3g); CARB 33.4g; FIB 2g; CHOL 0mg; IRON 1.7mg; SOD 9mg; CALC 36mg

Turkey Reubens are full of flavor without much fat.

Lemon Snaps

2 cups all-purpose flour
2 teaspoons baking powder
¼ teaspoon baking soda
1 cup sugar
1 tablespoon grated lemon rind, divided
½ teaspoon ground ginger
6½ tablespoons stick margarine, softened
2 teaspoons light-colored corn syrup
2 teaspoons vanilla extract
1 large egg
3 tablespoons sugar
Cooking spray

1. Preheat oven to 375°.

2. Combine all-purpose flour, baking powder, and baking soda in a medium bowl; stir mixture well, and set aside.

3. Place 1 cup sugar, 2 teaspoons lemon rind, and ginger in a food processor; process 1 minute or until lemon colored, scraping sides of processor bowl once.

4. Spoon sugar mixture into a large bowl; add softened margarine, and beat at medium speed of a mixer until light and fluffy. Add corn syrup, vanilla, and egg; beat well. Stir in flour mixture (dough will be stiff).

5. Combine remaining 1 teaspoon lemon rind and 3 tablespoons sugar in a bowl; stir well. Set lemon-sugar aside.

6. Coat hands lightly with cooking spray, and shape dough into 60 (1-inch) balls. Roll balls in lemon-sugar, and place 2 inches apart on baking sheets coated with cooking spray. Flatten balls with the bottom of a glass.

7. Bake at 375° for 7 minutes. Let cookies cool on pans 5 minutes. Remove from pans, and let cool completely on wire racks. Yield: 5 dozen (serving size: 2 cookies).

Note: Store remaining cookies in an airtight container at room temperature up to 1 week, or freeze up to 1 month.

Points: 2; **Exchanges:** 1 Starch, ½ Fat
Per serving: CAL 88 (29% from fat); PRO 1.2g; FAT 2.8g (sat 0.6g); CARB 14.8g; FIB 0.2g; CHOL 8mg; IRON 0.4mg; SOD 42mg; CALC 22mg

---

FLASH IN THE PAN

Serves 6

Turkey Reubens

Baked potato chips
(12 chips per person)

Molasses Crackles

Turkey Reubens

2¼ cups thinly sliced green cabbage
2 tablespoons fat-free Thousand Island dressing
2 tablespoons light mayonnaise
1 tablespoon Dijon mustard
12 (1-ounce) slices rye bread
6 ounces thinly sliced cooked turkey breast
6 (¾-ounce) slices fat-free Swiss processed cheese
Butter-flavored cooking spray

1. Combine first 3 ingredients in a bowl; toss well, and set aside.

2. Spread mustard evenly over 6 bread slices, and top with turkey slices. Top each with 1 cheese slice and ¼ cup cabbage mixture. Top with remaining bread slices.

3. Spray both sides of each sandwich with cooking spray; place sandwiches on a hot nonstick griddle or nonstick skillet coated with cooking spray. Cook on each side 2 minutes or until bread is lightly browned and cheese melts. Serve immediately. Yield: 6 servings.

Points: 5; **Exchanges:** 2 Very Lean Meat, 2½ Starch
Per serving: CAL 256 (12% from fat); PRO 19.8g; FAT 3.4g (sat 0.6g); CARB 36g; FIB 3.9g; CHOL 21mg; IRON 1.4mg; SOD 853mg; CALC 306mg

Molasses Crackles

2⅔ cups all-purpose flour
1¼ teaspoons baking powder
1 teaspoon ground ginger
¼ teaspoon baking soda
2¼ teaspoons ground cinnamon
¾ teaspoon ground cloves
⅛ teaspoon salt
½ cup dark molasses
7 tablespoons vegetable oil

2½ tablespoons dark corn syrup
¼   teaspoon grated orange rind
1⅓ cups sifted powdered sugar, divided
1   large egg
Cooking spray

1. Combine first 7 ingredients in a bowl; stir well, and set aside. Combine molasses, oil, corn syrup, and orange rind in a large bowl; beat at medium speed of a mixer until blended. Add 1 cup powdered sugar and egg; beat until well blended. Stir in flour mixture. Cover and freeze 1 hour.

2. Preheat oven to 375°.

3. Coat hands lightly with cooking spray, and shape dough into 48 (1-inch) balls. Roll balls in remaining powdered sugar; place 2 inches apart on baking sheets coated with cooking spray. Bake at 375° for 8 minutes. Let cool 2 minutes or until firm. Remove cookies from pans; let cool on wire racks. Yield: 4 dozen (serving size: 2 cookies).

Note: Store remaining cookies in an airtight container at room temperature up to 1 week, or freeze up to 1 month.

Points: 3; Exchanges: 1½ Starch, ½ Fat
Per serving: CAL 138 (23% from fat); PRO 1.8g; FAT 4.4g (sat 0.8g); CARB 23.4g; FIB 0.4g; CHOL 10mg; IRON 2mg; SOD 34mg; CALC 80mg

---

RAINY DAY LUNCH

Serves 6

Broccoli-Cheese-Stuffed Potatoes

Crispy Oatmeal Cookies

Broccoli-Cheese-Stuffed Potatoes

6   (8-ounce) baking potatoes
4   ounces Neufchâtel cheese (about ½ cup)
⅓   cup skim milk
¼   cup (2 ounces) crumbled blue cheese
2   large egg whites
1   cup chopped cooked broccoli
¼   cup sliced green onions
2   tablespoons grated Parmesan cheese
2   tablespoons dry breadcrumbs
2   teaspoons stick margarine, melted

1. Preheat oven to 400°.

2. Bake potatoes at 400° for 45 minutes or until done. Let cool slightly. Cut a ¼-inch-thick slice from the top of each potato, and discard. Carefully scoop out pulp, leaving shells intact. Set shells aside. Reduce oven temperature to 350°.

3. Place potato pulp in a large bowl, and mash; add Neufchâtel cheese, milk, and blue cheese. Beat at medium speed of a mixer 2 minutes or until smooth. Add egg whites; beat at medium speed until smooth. Stir in broccoli and green onions. Stuff shells with potato mixture.

4. Combine Parmesan cheese, breadcrumbs, and margarine; sprinkle mixture evenly over tops of potatoes. Place potatoes on a baking sheet; bake at 350° for 25 minutes or until thoroughly heated. Yield: 6 servings.

Points: 5; Exchanges: 2½ Starch, 1 Fat
Per serving: CAL 249 (29% from fat); PRO 10.4g; FAT 7.9g (sat 4.3g); CARB 35.5g; FIB 3.8g; CHOL 20mg; IRON 2.6mg; SOD 249mg; CALC 122mg

Crispy Oatmeal Cookies

½   cup stick margarine, softened
½   cup sugar
½   cup firmly packed brown sugar
½   cup egg substitute
1   teaspoon vanilla extract
1½ cups all-purpose flour
1   teaspoon baking powder
¾   teaspoon baking soda
¼   teaspoon salt
1¾ cups quick-cooking oats
1½ cups cornflakes
Cooking spray

1. Preheat oven to 350°.

2. Cream margarine; gradually add sugars, beating at medium speed of a mixer until light and fluffy. Add egg substitute and vanilla; beat well.

3. Combine flour and next 3 ingredients in a bowl; stir well. Add flour mixture to creamed mixture; beat well. Stir in oats and cornflakes.

4. Drop dough by level tablespoons, 2 inches apart, on baking sheets coated with cooking spray. Bake at 350° for 12 minutes. Remove from

Dash of ground nutmeg
3 cups low-fat vanilla ice cream

1. Combine bananas and lemon juice in a small bowl, and toss gently. Set aside. Melt margarine in a large nonstick skillet over medium heat; stir in honey, grated lemon rind, and nutmeg. Add banana mixture, and cook 2 minutes or until banana is slightly soft, basting frequently with honey mixture.

2. Spoon ½ cup vanilla ice cream into each of 6 dessert bowls. Spoon warm banana mixture evenly over each serving. Serve immediately. Yield: 6 servings.

Points: 3; **Exchanges:** 1 Fruit, 1 Starch, ½ Fat
Per serving: CAL 158 (22% from fat); PRO 3.1g; FAT 3.8g (sat 2g); CARB 29.9g; FIB 1.4g; CHOL 9mg; IRON 0.2mg; SOD 65mg; CALC 95mg

---

DOWN-HOME FAVORITES

Serves 6

Parsleyed Meat Loaf

Macaroni-and-Cheese Casserole

Steamed green beans
(1 cup per person)

Old-fashioned Banana Pudding

Parsleyed Meat Loaf

To make sandwiches, slice leftover meat loaf and place on whole-wheat bread with mayonnaise, lettuce, and cheddar cheese.

2 pounds ground round
1¼ cups regular oats
1 cup chopped fresh parsley
¾ cup chopped onion
¼ cup egg substitute
2 tablespoons chopped green bell pepper
½ teaspoon salt
½ teaspoon dried thyme
½ teaspoon black pepper
¼ teaspoon ground allspice
⅛ teaspoon ground nutmeg
⅛ teaspoon ground red pepper
1 large garlic clove, minced
Cooking spray
¼ cup ketchup

1. Preheat oven to 350°.

2. Combine first 13 ingredients in a large bowl; stir well. Shape mixture into a 9- x 5-inch loaf; place loaf on a broiler pan coated with cooking spray. Bake at 350° for 1 hour and 15 minutes. Spread ketchup evenly over meat loaf; bake an additional 5 minutes. Let stand 5 minutes before serving. Yield: 10 servings.

Points: 4; **Exchanges:** 2½ Lean Meat, ½ Starch
Per serving: CAL 188 (30% from fat); PRO 22g; FAT 6.2g (sat 2.1g); CARB 10.1g; FIB 1.6g; CHOL 56mg; IRON 2.8mg; SOD 244mg; CALC 22mg

Macaroni-and-Cheese Casserole

6 ounces uncooked elbow macaroni
Cooking spray
1 teaspoon vegetable oil
1 cup chopped onion
1 cup chopped green bell pepper
1 cup (4 ounces) shredded reduced-fat cheddar cheese
1 cup fat-free mayonnaise
¼ teaspoon pepper
1 (10¾-ounce) can reduced-fat reduced-sodium cream of celery soup, undiluted
1 (4-ounce) can sliced mushrooms, drained
1 (2-ounce) jar diced pimiento, undrained
1 cup cornflakes cereal, crushed

1. Preheat oven to 350°.

2. Cook macaroni according to package directions, omitting salt and fat; drain. Rinse macaroni under cold water; drain well, and set aside.

3. Coat a large nonstick skillet with cooking spray; add vegetable oil, and place over medium heat until hot. Add onion and bell pepper, and sauté until tender.

4. Combine sautéed vegetables, macaroni, cheese, and next 5 ingredients in a large bowl; stir well. Spoon into a 2-quart casserole coated with cooking spray. Sprinkle crushed cereal over casserole. Bake, uncovered, at 350° for 40 minutes. Yield: 6 servings.

Points: 5; **Exchanges:** ½ Med-fat Meat, 2½ Starch
Per serving: CAL 258 (21% from fat); PRO 10.6g; FAT 6g (sat 3g); CARB 40.6g; FIB 2g; CHOL 14mg; IRON 2mg; SOD 938mg; CALC 204mg

The simplest of fruits, lemon adds a sophisticated touch to any dish, whether sweet or savory. Here are a few tips to keep in mind when you're cooking with this citrus fruit.

• When shopping for lemons, choose firm ones that feel heavy for their size.

• The skin should be smooth and brightly colored with no soft or green spots.

•Unrefrigerated lemons will keep for several days.

• Lemons stored in a plastic bag in the refrigerator will keep for up to a month.

•Lemons are much easier to squeeze and will yield more juice if they are at room temperature. If you have stored the lemons in the refrigerator, heat them one at a time in the microwave at HIGH for 20 to 40 seconds or just until they are warm to the touch. Then roll the lemons firmly on the countertop to soften them.

Old-fashioned Banana Pudding

⅓ cup firmly packed brown sugar
1½ tablespoons cornstarch
1⅔ cups skim milk
⅓ cup egg substitute
1 tablespoon margarine
1 teaspoon vanilla extract
26 vanilla wafers
3 medium bananas, peeled and sliced
  (about 2 cups)
3 large egg whites
2 tablespoons sugar

1. Combine brown sugar and cornstarch in a medium saucepan; gradually add milk, stirring constantly with a whisk until blended. Bring to a boil over medium heat, and cook 1 minute, stirring constantly. Gradually stir about one-fourth of hot milk mixture into egg substitute, and add to remaining hot mixture; cook 3 minutes or until thick, stirring constantly. Remove from heat; add margarine and vanilla, stirring until margarine melts. Pour into a bowl; let cool completely.

2. Arrange half of vanilla wafers in bottom of a 2-quart casserole; top with half of banana slices and half of custard. Repeat layers once with remaining vanilla wafers, banana slices, and custard.

3. Preheat oven to 325°.

4. Beat egg whites at high speed of a mixer until soft peaks form. Gradually add 2 tablespoons sugar, beating until stiff peaks form. Spread meringue over custard, sealing to edge of dish. Bake at 325° for 25 minutes or until golden. Serve warm or chilled.

Points: 6; **Exchanges:** 1 Fat, 2 Starch, 1 Fruit
Per serving: CAL 273 (22% from fat); PRO 6.9g; FAT 6.6g (sat 1.2g); CARB 47.2g; FIB 1.7g; CHOL 1mg; IRON 1.1mg; SOD 190mg; CALC 112mg

---

BURGERS ON THE GRILL

Serves 6

Mushroom Burgers

Creamy Potato Salad

Vegetable Packets

Mushroom Burgers

1½ pounds ground round
1½ cups finely chopped mushrooms
¼ cup finely chopped onion
1 tablespoon chili powder
½ teaspoon salt
6 tablespoons reduced-calorie ketchup
6 (1½-ounce) whole-wheat hamburger buns
6 curly leaf lettuce leaves
6 (¼-inch-thick) slices tomato
6 (¼-inch-thick) slices red onion

1. Combine first 5 ingredients in a large bowl, and stir well. Shape mixture into 6 (½-inch-thick) patties. Prepare grill or broiler. Place patties on grill rack or broiler pan, and cook 5 minutes on each side or until done.

2. Spread 1 tablespoon ketchup over bottom half of each bun; top each with beef patty, lettuce leaf, tomato slice, onion slice, and top half of bun. Yield: 6 servings.

Points: 7; **Exchanges:** 3 Lean Meat, 2 Starch, 1 Veg
Per serving: CAL 344 (29% from fat); PRO 30g; FAT 11g (sat 3.6g); CARB 30.5g; FIB 3.2g; CHOL 87mg; IRON 4mg; SOD 575mg; CALC 48mg

Creamy Potato Salad

3 cups peeled cooked cubed red potato
  (about 1 pound)
2 tablespoons chopped green onions
1 (2-ounce) jar diced pimiento, drained
¼ cup fat-free mayonnaise
¼ cup plain fat-free yogurt
1 tablespoon prepared mustard
1½ teaspoons sugar
1½ teaspoons white wine vinegar
¼ teaspoon salt
¼ teaspoon celery seeds
⅛ teaspoon garlic powder
⅛ teaspoon pepper

1. Combine first 3 ingredients in a large bowl, and toss gently. Combine mayonnaise and next 8 ingredients in a small bowl; stir well. Pour dressing over salad; toss gently to coat. Cover and chill. Yield: 6 servings (½ cup serving).

Points: 1; **Exchanges:** 1 Starch
Per serving: CAL 85 (3% from fat); PRO 2g; FAT 0.3g (sat 0g); CARB 19.1g; FIB 1.2g; CHOL 0mg; IRON 0.5mg; SOD 269mg; CALC 30mg

Mushroom Burgers,
Creamy Potato Salad,
and Vegetable Packets

Vegetable Packets

1½ cups sliced yellow squash
1½ cups sliced zucchini
1½ cups cauliflower florets
1½ cups broccoli florets
1   cup thinly sliced carrot
1   medium onion, thinly sliced
⅔ cup fat-free Italian dressing
½ teaspoon dried basil
¼ teaspoon salt
¼ teaspoon pepper

1. Combine first 6 ingredients in a large bowl; toss gently. Combine dressing, basil, salt, and pepper in a small bowl; stir well. Pour dressing mixture over vegetables; toss gently to coat.

2. Divide vegetable mixture evenly among 6 large squares of heavy-duty foil. Wrap vegetables securely, sealing edges of foil packets.

3. Prepare grill. Place packets on grill rack; cook 4 minutes or until crisp-tender, turning packets once. Yield: 6 servings.

Indulge in Oven-Fried Catfish, Marinated Coleslaw, sliced tomatoes, and Baked Hush Puppies for less than 400 calories per serving.

Note: Packets may be cooked in a preheated 450° oven for 15 minutes or until crisp-tender without turning, if desired.

Points: 0; **Exchanges**: 2 Veg
Per serving: CAL 56 (5% from fat); PRO 2.5g; FAT 0.3g (sat 0.1g); CARB 12.2g; FIB 3.3g; CHOL 0mg; IRON 0.8mg; SOD 358mg; CALC 43mg

MISSISSIPPI FISH "FRY"

Serves 8

Oven-Fried Catfish

Marinated Coleslaw

Sliced tomatoes
(2 slices per person)

Baked Hush Puppies

Watermelon wedges
(flesh equivalent to 2 cups
cubed per person)

Oven-Fried Catfish

6   (1-ounce) slices French bread, cubed
¼   cup fat-free mayonnaise
4   teaspoons water
8   (6-ounce) dressed catfish
Cooking spray
Lemon wedges (optional)
Parsley sprigs (optional)

1. Preheat oven to 350°.

2. Place bread cubes in a food processor, and process 30 seconds or until breadcrumbs are fine. Sprinkle breadcrumbs onto a baking sheet; bake at 350° for 5 minutes or until lightly browned. Place breadcrumbs in a shallow dish; set aside. Increase oven temperature to 450°.

3. Combine mayonnaise and water in a shallow bowl; stir well. Dip fish, 1 at a time, in mayonnaise mixture; dredge in breadcrumbs. Place fish on a baking sheet coated with cooking spray. Bake at 450° for 15 minutes or until fish flakes easily when tested with a fork. Serve with lemon wedges, and garnish with parsley sprigs, if desired. Yield: 8 servings.

Points: 4; **Exchanges:** 3 Very Lean Meat, 1 Starch
Per serving: CAL 197 (24% from fat); PRO 22g; FAT 5.2g (sat 1.2g); CARB 13.3g; FIB 0.5g; CHOL 65mg; IRON 1.5mg; SOD 298mg; CALC 53mg

Marinated Coleslaw

3½ cups thinly sliced green cabbage
1¼ cups thinly sliced red cabbage
1   cup coarsely shredded carrot
1   cup diced celery
½   cup chopped onion
¾   cup cider vinegar
¼   cup sugar
1½ tablespoons vegetable oil
¾   teaspoon dry mustard
½   teaspoon ground turmeric
½   teaspoon celery seeds
Small red cabbage leaves (optional)

1. Combine cabbages, carrot, celery, and onion in a large bowl; toss gently, and set aside. Combine vinegar and next 5 ingredients in a small saucepan; bring to a boil over medium heat. Cook until sugar dissolves, stirring occasionally.

Pour hot vinegar mixture over cabbage mixture, and toss gently to coat. Cover and marinate in refrigerator at least 8 hours, stirring occasionally. Serve with a slotted spoon in cabbage leaves, if desired. Yield: 8 servings (serving size: ¾ cup).

Points: 1; **Exchanges:** 1 Veg, ½ Fat, ½ Starch
Per serving: CAL 73 (36% from fat); PRO 0.9g; FAT 2.9g (sat 0.5g); CARB 12.5g; FIB 1.7g; CHOL 0mg; IRON 0.6mg; SOD 26mg; CALC 36mg

Baked Hush Puppies

⅔   cup yellow cornmeal
½   cup minced fresh onion
⅓   cup all-purpose flour
1   teaspoon baking powder
½   teaspoon salt
⅓   cup skim milk
¼   cup egg substitute
1   tablespoon vegetable oil
⅛   teaspoon pepper
Cooking spray

1. Preheat oven to 450°.

2. Combine first 5 ingredients in a medium bowl; make a well in center of mixture. Combine milk, egg substitute, oil, and pepper; add to cornmeal mixture, stirring just until moist.

3. Divide batter evenly among miniature (1¾-inch) muffin cups coated with cooking spray. Bake at 450° for 12 minutes or until lightly browned. Remove hush puppies from pans immediately. Serve warm. Yield: 2 dozen (serving size: 3 hush puppies).

Points: 2; **Exchanges:** 1 Starch
Per serving: CAL 93 (26% from fat); PRO 2.7g; FAT 2.7g (sat 0.6g); CARB 14.4g; FIB 0.9g; CHOL 0mg; IRON 0.9mg; SOD 201mg; CALC 54mg

---

**JUST LIKE MOM
USED TO MAKE**

Serves 6

Onion-Topped Pot Roast

Sugar-and-Spice Baked Apples

Whole-Wheat Yeast Biscuits

Onion-Topped Pot Roast

Lean cuts of meat such as round roast need to be marinated, simmered for long periods of time, or cooked in wine or citrus juices to make them tender.

1 (2-pound) lean, boned bottom round roast
Cooking spray
¼ teaspoon pepper
2 garlic cloves
1 cup coarsely chopped onion
½ cup dry red wine
½ cup no-salt-added beef broth, undiluted
¼ cup no-salt-added tomato juice
½ teaspoon salt
1 cup water
18 small round red potatoes (about 1½ pounds)
18 baby carrots (about ½ pound)

1. Trim fat from roast. Coat an ovenproof Dutch oven with cooking spray; place over medium-high heat until hot. Add roast, and brown on all sides. Remove roast from Dutch oven, and sprinkle with pepper; set roast aside. Wipe drippings from pan with a paper towel.

2. Drop garlic through food chute with food processor on, and process 5 seconds. Drop onion through food chute; process 1 minute or until smooth. Spread onion-garlic purée over roast. Return roast to Dutch oven. Bake, uncovered, at 350° for 1 hour.

3. Add wine and next 3 ingredients to pan; cover and bake 2½ hours. Add 1 cup water, potatoes, and carrots; cover and bake 1 additional hour or until roast is tender.

4. Place roast and vegetables on a large platter, and serve with gravy. Yield: 6 servings (serving size: 3 ounces roast, 3 carrots, 3 potatoes, and 2 tablespoons gravy).

Points: 6; **Exchanges:** 3½ Very Lean Meat, 2 Starch
Per serving: CAL 293 (17% from fat); PRO 33.1g; FAT 5.6g (sat 2g); CARB 26.4g; FIB 3.8g; CHOL 74mg; IRON 4.6mg; SOD 288mg; CALC 39mg

Sugar-and-Spice Baked Apples

6 medium Gala or other red cooking apples
6 tablespoons raisins
¼ cup firmly packed brown sugar
½ teaspoon ground cinnamon
½ teaspoon ground nutmeg
2 tablespoons reduced-calorie stick margarine
1 cup apple juice

1. Preheat oven to 350°.

2. Core apples to within ½ inch from bottom, and peel top third of each apple. Combine raisins and next 3 ingredients in a small bowl; stir well. Spoon raisin mixture evenly into cavity of each apple. Place apples in a 10- x 6-inch baking dish, and top each apple with 1 teaspoon margarine. Pour apple juice evenly over apples. Cover and bake at 350° for 35 minutes or until apples are tender, basting occasionally with juice. Yield: 6 servings.

Points: 3; **Exchanges:** 2½ Fruit, ½ Fat, ½ Starch
Per serving: CAL 206 (14% from fat); PRO 0.6g; FAT 3.2g (sat 0.5g); CARB 47.8g; FIB 6.1g; CHOL 0mg; IRON 0.9mg; SOD 42mg; CALC 30mg

Microwave Directions: Prepare apples as directed. Cover with heavy-duty plastic wrap, and vent. Microwave at HIGH 10 to 12 minutes or until apples are tender, basting with juice and rotating dish a quarter-turn every 2 minutes. Let stand, covered, 5 minutes before serving.

Whole-Wheat Yeast Biscuits

1 package dry yeast
¼ cup warm water (105° to 115°)
1¾ cups plus 2 tablespoons all-purpose flour
¾ cup whole-wheat flour
1 tablespoon sugar
1 teaspoon baking powder
½ teaspoon baking soda
¼ teaspoon salt
3 tablespoons chilled reduced-calorie stick margarine, cut into small pieces
⅔ cup low-fat buttermilk
2 tablespoons all-purpose flour
Cooking spray

1. Dissolve yeast in warm water in a small bowl, and let stand 5 minutes.

2. Combine 1¾ cups plus 2 tablespoons all-purpose flour and next 5 ingredients in a bowl; cut in margarine with a pastry blender or 2 knives until mixture resembles coarse meal. Add yeast mixture and buttermilk, stirring just until moist. Cover and chill 8 hours.

3. Preheat oven to 425°.

4. Sprinkle 2 tablespoons all-purpose flour evenly over work surface. Turn dough out onto floured surface, and knead for 1 minute. Roll dough to a ½-inch thickness on floured surface; cut with a 2-inch biscuit cutter. Place biscuits on a baking sheet coated with cooking spray. Bake at 425° for 10 minutes or until golden. Yield: 16 biscuits (serving size: 1 biscuit).

Note: Store leftover biscuits in an airtight container up to 2 days. To reheat, wrap tightly in foil, and bake in a preheated 350° oven for 15 minutes or until warm.

Points: 2; **Exchanges:** 1 Starch
Per serving: CAL 82 (19% from fat); PRO 2.5g; FAT 1.7g (sat 0.3g); CARB 14.5g; FIB 1.2g; CHOL 0mg; IRON 0.8mg; SOD 113mg; CALC 27mg

FAST FAMILY SUPPER

Serves 4

Pork Chops With Maple-Pecan Sauce

Garlic Mashed Potatoes

Steamed broccoli
(1 cup per person)

Chocolate-Mocha Pudding

Pork Chops With Maple-Pecan Sauce

4	(4-ounce) lean boned center-cut loin pork chops
2	teaspoons Dijon mustard
2	tablespoons all-purpose flour
½	teaspoon ground ginger
Cooking spray	
2	teaspoons vegetable oil
2	tablespoons reduced-calorie maple syrup
1	tablespoon chopped pecans, toasted
Celery leaves (optional)	

1. Trim fat from chops. Place chops between 2 sheets of heavy-duty plastic wrap, and flatten to a ¼-inch thickness using a meat mallet or rolling pin. Spread mustard on both sides of chops. Combine flour and ginger in a shallow dish; stir well. Dredge pork chops in flour mixture.

2. Coat a nonstick skillet with cooking spray; add oil, and place over medium heat until hot. Add chops, and cook 3 minutes on each side or until chops are browned. Combine maple syrup and pecans; drizzle over pork chops. Cover and cook 4 minutes or until chops are tender, turning once.

3. Arrange chops on a serving platter, and drizzle with pan drippings. Garnish with celery leaves, if desired. Yield: 4 servings.

Points: 6; **Exchanges:** 3 Lean Meat, ½ Starch, ½ Fat
Per serving: CAL 234 (46% from fat); PRO 25.5g; FAT 11.9g (sat 3.3g); CARB 4.4g; FIB 0.2g; CHOL 71mg; IRON 1.1mg; SOD 151mg; CALC 7mg

Garlic Mashed Potatoes

4½	cups peeled cubed baking potato
4	garlic cloves
1	bay leaf

Pork Chops With Maple-Pecan Sauce offers lots of flavor with little effort.

Simple Baked Chicken, Basil Mashed Potatoes with Home-style Gravy, and Stewed Tomatoes and Onions bring back comfortable memories.

¾ cup plain low-fat yogurt
½ cup skim milk
¼ teaspoon salt

1. Place potato, garlic, and bay leaf in a saucepan, and cover with water; bring to a boil. Cover, reduce heat, and simmer 15 minutes or until tender.
2. Drain mixture, and discard bay leaf. Return potato and garlic to pan, and beat at medium speed of a mixer until mashed. Add yogurt, milk, and salt; beat just until blended. Yield: 4 servings (serving size: 1 cup).

Points: 2; Exchanges: 2 Starch
Per serving: CAL 143 (6% from fat); PRO 7.9g; FAT 0.9g (sat 0.5g); CARB 27g; FIB 3.1g; CHOL 3mg; IRON 5.7mg; SOD 210mg; CALC 174mg

Chocolate-Mocha Pudding

½ cup sugar
⅓ cup unsweetened cocoa
2 tablespoons plus 2 teaspoons cornstarch
1½ cups 1% low-fat milk
½ cup brewed coffee
1 teaspoon vanilla extract
¼ cup frozen reduced-calorie whipped topping, thawed

1. Combine first 3 ingredients in a medium saucepan; stir well. Gradually add milk and coffee, stirring with a whisk until blended. Bring to a boil over medium heat, and cook 1 minute or until thick, stirring constantly. Remove from heat, and stir in vanilla.
2. Spoon chocolate mixture evenly into 4 (6-ounce) custard cups; top each serving with 1 tablespoon whipped topping. Yield: 4 servings.

Points: 4; Exchanges: 2½ Starch
Per serving: CAL 199 (11% from fat); PRO 5.2g; FAT 2.5g (sat 1.2g); CARB 38.9g; FIB 0g; CHOL 4mg; IRON 1.4mg; SOD 53mg; CALC 128mg

Serves 6

Simple Baked Chicken
Basil Mashed Potatoes
Home-style Gravy
Stewed Tomatoes and Onions

Simple Baked Chicken

1   (3-pound) chicken, cut up and skinned
Cooking spray
½   cup thawed lemonade concentrate, undiluted
2   tablespoons low-salt chicken broth
½   teaspoon garlic powder
1   teaspoon dried rosemary, crushed
1   teaspoon freshly ground pepper

1. Preheat oven to 400°.

2. Place chicken on a broiler pan coated with cooking spray. Combine lemonade concentrate, chicken broth, and garlic powder; stir well. Sprinkle chicken with rosemary and pepper; brush lightly with lemonade mixture.

3. Bake at 400° for 45 minutes or until chicken is done, turning and basting occasionally with lemonade mixture. Yield: 6 servings (serving size: 3 ounces chicken).

Points: 5; **Exchanges:** 2 Lean Meat, 1½ Very Lean Meat, 1 Starch
Per serving: CAL 235 (29% from fat); PRO 28.6g; FAT 7.5g (sat 2g); CARB 12.1g; FIB 0.2g; CHOL 87mg; IRON 1.6mg; SOD 87mg; CALC 21mg

Basil Mashed Potatoes

Basil adds an updated twist to an age-old favorite.

2½   cups peeled cubed baking potato
3   tablespoons skim milk
2   tablespoons plain fat-free yogurt
¼   teaspoon salt
⅛   teaspoon ground white pepper
1½   tablespoons minced fresh or 1½ teaspoons dried basil
Basil sprigs (optional)

1. Place potato in a saucepan, and cover with water; bring to a boil. Cook 15 minutes or until tender; drain. Return potato to pan; beat at medium speed of a mixer 1 minute or until smooth. Add milk and next 3 ingredients; beat well. Stir in basil. Spoon into a serving bowl; garnish with basil sprigs, if desired. Yield: 6 servings (serving size: ½ cup).

Points: 1; **Exchanges:** 1 Starch
Per serving: CAL 68 (1% from fat); PRO 2.2g; FAT 0.1g (sat 0g); CARB 15g; FIB 1.3g; CHOL 0mg; IRON 0.6mg; SOD 110mg; CALC 27mg

Home-style Gravy

This virtually fat-free gravy is the perfect accompaniment to baked chicken, roasted pork, or mashed potatoes.

1½   tablespoons cornstarch
¼   cup water
1¼   cups low-salt chicken broth
Cooking spray
½   cup chopped onion
1   teaspoon dried thyme
¼   teaspoon salt
¼   teaspoon poultry seasoning
¼   teaspoon pepper

1. Combine cornstarch and water in a small bowl; stir with a whisk until blended. Stir in broth, and set aside.

2. Coat a medium saucepan with cooking spray; place over medium-high heat until hot. Add onion and thyme, and sauté 3 minutes or until tender. Stir in cornstarch mixture, salt, poultry seasoning, and pepper. Bring to a boil over medium heat, and cook 1 minute or until thick and bubbly, stirring constantly. Yield: 1½ cups (serving size: 1 tablespoon).

Points: 0; **Exchanges:** Free
Per serving: CAL 5 (18% from fat); PRO 0.2g; FAT 0.1g (sat 0g); CARB 0.9g; FIB 0.1g; CHOL 0mg; IRON 0.2mg; SOD 29mg; CALC 2mg

Stewed Tomatoes and Onions

Good summer tomatoes are the key ingredient for this recipe.

Cooking spray
½   cup chopped green bell pepper
1   small onion, thinly sliced and separated into rings

¼ cup thinly sliced celery
1 garlic clove, minced
3 cups peeled coarsely chopped tomato
1 tablespoon red wine vinegar
2 teaspoons sugar
⅛ teaspoon pepper

1. Coat a large nonstick skillet with cooking spray; place over medium-high heat until hot. Add bell pepper, onion, celery, and garlic; sauté 5 minutes or until vegetables are tender. Add chopped tomato and remaining ingredients; bring mixture to a boil. Cover, reduce heat, and simmer 15 minutes, stirring occasionally. Yield: 6 servings (serving size: ½ cup).

Points: 0; **Exchanges:** 2 Veg
Per serving: CAL 37 (12% from fat); PRO 1.2; FAT 0.5g (sat 0.1g); CARB 8.3g; FIB 1.8g; CHOL 0mg; IRON 0.7mg; SOD 14mg; CALC 11mg

---

WARMING WINTER SUPPER

Serves 8

Barbecue Pork Stew

Chile-Cheese Cornbread

Apple-Raisin Crumble

Barbecue Pork Stew

Slowly simmering this stew tenderizes the pork and blends the flavors.

1½ pounds lean, boned pork loin, cubed
½ cup all-purpose flour
Cooking spray
1 teaspoon vegetable oil
2½ cups chopped onion
2½ cups peeled diced baking potato
⅔ cup water
¼ cup firmly packed brown sugar
1 tablespoon paprika
3 tablespoons cider vinegar
3 tablespoons reduced-calorie ketchup
2 tablespoons low-sodium Worcestershire sauce
2 teaspoons garlic powder
2 teaspoons chili powder
1 teaspoon freshly ground pepper
½ teaspoon salt
1 bay leaf
1 (14½-ounce) can no-salt-added whole tomatoes, undrained and chopped

1 (8-ounce) can no-salt-added tomato sauce
2 (15-ounce) cans no-salt-added kidney beans, undrained

1. Combine pork and flour in a zip-top plastic bag. Seal bag, and shake to coat pork.

2. Coat a large Dutch oven with cooking spray; add oil, and place over medium heat until hot. Add pork and onion; cook until onion is crisp-tender. Stir in potato and next 13 ingredients; bring to a boil. Cover, reduce heat, and simmer 1½ hours or until pork is tender, stirring occasionally. Stir in beans, and cook until thoroughly heated. Discard bay leaf. Yield: 8 servings (serving size: 1½ cups).

Points: 8; **Exchanges:** 2½ Lean Meat, 3 Starch, 2 Veg
Per serving: CAL 418 (17% from fat); PRO 30.2g; FAT 8g (sat 2.5g); CARB 57.3g; FIB 7.1g; CHOL 51mg; IRON 5.4mg; SOD 246mg; CALC 76mg

Chile-Cheese Cornbread

1 cup yellow cornmeal
1 cup all-purpose flour
¼ cup nonfat dry milk powder
4 teaspoons baking powder
1 tablespoon sugar
¼ teaspoon salt
1 cup water
½ cup egg substitute
2 tablespoons vegetable oil
¾ cup (3 ounces) shredded reduced-fat cheddar cheese
1 (4.5-ounce) can chopped green chiles, drained
Cooking spray

1. Preheat oven to 375°.

2. Combine first 6 ingredients in a medium bowl, and make a well in center of mixture. Combine water, egg substitute, and oil; add to cornmeal mixture, stirring just until moist. Stir in cheese and green chiles.

3. Pour batter into an 8-inch square baking dish coated with cooking spray. Bake at 375° for 30 minutes or until golden. Yield: 16 servings.

Points: 2; **Exchanges:** 1 Starch, ½ Lean Meat
Per serving: CAL 107 (25% from fat); PRO 4.6g; FAT 3g (sat 0.9g); CARB 15.3g; FIB 0.7g; CHOL 4mg; IRON 1mg; SOD 125mg; CALC 98mg

Apple-Raisin Crumble

We used Rome apples in our test kitchen, but any other mildly tart to sweet cooking apple may be substituted.

4½ cups peeled coarsely chopped Rome apple
½ cup raisins
⅓ cup apple juice
⅓ cup sugar
2 tablespoons all-purpose flour
½ teaspoon ground cinnamon
¼ teaspoon ground nutmeg
Cooking spray
⅔ cup quick-cooking oats
¼ cup all-purpose flour
¼ cup firmly packed brown sugar
¼ cup chilled reduced-calorie stick
    margarine, cut into small pieces

1. Preheat oven to 375°.

2. Combine apple, raisins, and apple juice in a large bowl; toss gently. Combine ⅓ cup sugar, 2 tablespoons all-purpose flour, ground cinnamon, and nutmeg; sprinkle over apple mixture, and toss gently to coat.

3. Coat an 8-inch square baking pan with cooking spray. Spoon apple mixture into pan. Combine quick-cooking oats, ¼ cup all-purpose flour, and ¼ cup brown sugar in a small bowl; cut in margarine with a pastry blender or 2 knives until mixture resembles coarse meal. Sprinkle oat mixture evenly over apple mixture. Bake at 375° for 40 minutes or until apple is tender and oat mixture is lightly browned. Serve warm. Yield: 8 servings.

Points: 4; **Exchanges:** 2 Fruit, 1 Starch, ½ Fat
Per serving: CAL 219 (18% from fat); PRO 2g; FAT 4.5g (sat 0.7g); CARB 45.8g; FIB 3.8g; CHOL 0mg; IRON 1mg; SOD 59mg; CALC 21mg

Because canned green chiles are mild, Chile-Cheese Cornbread ranks low on the heat scale.

SOUTHWESTERN FIESTA

Serves 6

Southwest Hopping John

Green salad

(1 cup mixed salad greens with 1
tablespoon fat-free dressing per person)

Individual Caramel Flans

Southwest Hopping John

This Southern dish of black-eyed peas, pork, and
rice gets a Southwestern twist with cumin and
jalapeño peppers.

Cooking spray
1½ cups chopped onion
1½ cups chopped green bell pepper
1   teaspoon ground cumin
2   garlic cloves, minced
1   (16-ounce) package frozen black-eyed
    peas
2   cups low-salt chicken broth

**Serve Individual
Caramel Flans with
fresh fruit such as
grapes, strawberries,
and kiwifruit.**

1   cup light beer
¾   cup uncooked long-grain brown rice
¼   pound diced lean, lower salt ham
2   teaspoons minced jalapeño pepper
¼   teaspoon salt
2   cups seeded diced tomato
Toasted Cornbread Triangles

1. Coat a Dutch oven with cooking spray, and place over medium-high heat until hot. Add onion, bell pepper, cumin, and garlic; sauté until tender. Stir in black-eyed peas and next 6 ingredients; bring to a boil. Cover, reduce heat, and simmer 45 minutes or until peas and rice are tender. Remove from heat, and stir in diced tomato. Serve with Toasted Cornbread Triangles. Yield: 6 servings.

TOASTED CORNBREAD TRIANGLES:
½   cup all-purpose flour
½   cup yellow cornmeal
½   teaspoon baking powder
⅛   teaspoon salt
1   tablespoon sugar
¾   cup low-fat buttermilk
2   large egg whites, lightly beaten
Butter-flavored cooking spray

1. Preheat oven to 350°.

2. Combine flour, cornmeal, baking powder, salt, and sugar in a bowl. Combine buttermilk and egg whites; add to dry ingredients, stirring just until moist. Pour into a 9-inch square baking pan coated with cooking spray. Bake at 350° for 15 minutes or until golden. Let cool completely in pan on a wire rack.

3. Cut cornbread into 12 squares; cut each square into 2 triangles. Place triangles on a baking sheet; lightly coat with cooking spray. Broil 1 minute or until lightly browned. Turn cornbread triangles over, and lightly coat with cooking spray. Broil an additional minute or until lightly browned. Yield: 24 triangles.

Points: 7; **Exchanges:** 4 Starch, ½ Very Lean Meat, 1 Veg
Per serving: CAL 373 (8% from fat); PRO 18g; FAT 3.3g (sat 0.8g); CARB 68.1g; FIB 5.1g; CHOL 9mg; IRON 4.1mg; SOD 388mg; CALC 100mg

Individual Caramel Flans

When turned out onto a serving plate, this Spanish baked custard is automatically glazed with the caramel from the custard cup.

¾   cup sugar, divided
Cooking spray
1   (12-ounce) can evaporated skim milk
½   cup skim milk
¾   cup egg substitute
⅛   teaspoon salt
½   teaspoon almond extract
2   cups assorted fresh fruit

1. Place ½ cup sugar in a small heavy saucepan over medium heat; cook until sugar dissolves, stirring constantly. Continue cooking an additional 5 minutes or until golden, stirring frequently. Immediately pour into 6 (6-ounce) custard cups coated with cooking spray, tipping quickly until caramelized sugar coats bottom of cups, and set aside.

2. Preheat oven to 325°.

3. Combine milks in a medium saucepan, and cook over medium-high heat to 180° or until tiny bubbles form around edge (do not boil). Remove from heat.

4. Combine egg substitute, remaining ¼ cup sugar, salt, and almond extract in a medium bowl; stir well with a whisk. Gradually stir about 1 cup hot milk into egg mixture; add to remaining hot milk, stirring constantly. Pour mixture evenly into custard cups; cover each cup with foil. Place cups in a shallow pan; pour hot water into pan to a depth of 1 inch. Bake at 325° for 40 minutes or until a knife inserted near center comes out clean. Remove cups from water; let cool slightly. Cover surface of custard with plastic wrap, and chill at least 8 hours.

5. Loosen edges of custard with a knife or rubber spatula; invert onto individual plates. Arrange ⅓ cup assorted fresh fruit around each flan. Yield: 6 servings.

Points: 5; **Exchanges:** ½ Lean Meat, ½ Sk Milk, 2 Starch
Per serving: CAL 228 (15% from fat); PRO 8.9g; FAT 3.7g (sat 0.7g); CARB 41g; FIB 1.3g; CHOL 3mg; IRON 0.9mg; SOD 189mg; CALC 224mg

Some Enchanted Evening

CULTIVATE YOUR ARTISTIC SIDE
WITH THESE ELEGANT MEALS.

Chefs have a reputation for being a pretty original crowd. They are artists, after all. Indeed, cooking, in some circles, is referred to as the culinary arts, and you don't have to own a restaurant or write a cookbook to know that the perfect meal placed on the perfect plate is a masterpiece in the making. There's no better opportunity to prove your Picasso potential than a special occasion with friends.

But it's hard to chat and bond with the guests (even if "the guest" is your significant other who just landed the world's best promotion) when you're in the kitchen looking like something out of Edvard Munch's Scream. Imagination may be the master of art, but sometimes even the most creative among us runs out of ideas. With that in mind, we've designed eight menus to get you out of the kitchen and into the living room. These simplified meals centered around dishes such as Chicken Cacciatore and Garlic-Sage Cornish Hens With Wild Rice are perfect for special occasions and they won't require you to work especially hard. Because, as any artist will attest, you have to experience life to create art.

Lemon Cream Tart is just that—tart, not cloyingly sweet.

Chicken Cacciatore

Serves 4

Chicken Cacciatore

Chilled Asparagus With
Feta Vinaigrette

Lemon Cream Tart

Chicken Cacciatore

Spoon over hot cooked pasta, such as rotini.

- 1 pound skinned, boned chicken thighs, cut into 1-inch cubes
- 1 cup sliced mushrooms
- ¾ cup sliced zucchini
- ½ cup chopped green bell pepper
- ½ cup chopped onion
- 1 teaspoon olive oil
- 1 large garlic clove, minced
- 2 (8-ounce) cans no-salt-added tomato sauce
- ¼ cup dry red wine
- 1 tablespoon chopped fresh or 1 teaspoon dried oregano
- ½ teaspoon salt
- 1½ teaspoons chopped fresh or ½ teaspoon dried thyme
- ¼ teaspoon pepper

Oregano sprigs (optional)
Thyme sprigs (optional)

1. Put chicken in 2-quart casserole; cover with wax paper. Microwave at HIGH 5 to 6 minutes, stirring after 4 minutes. Drain; set aside. Wipe dish dry.

2. Combine mushrooms and next 5 ingredients in dish; toss well. Microwave, uncovered, at HIGH 4 minutes, stirring after 2 minutes. Add tomato sauce and next 5 ingredients; stir well. Microwave at HIGH 8 to 12 minutes or until slightly thick, stirring every 4 minutes. Return chicken to dish; stir well. Microwave at HIGH 6 minutes or until chicken is thoroughly heated, stirring after 3 minutes. Let stand 3 minutes. Garnish with oregano and thyme sprigs, if desired. Yield: 4 servings (serving size: 1 cup).

Points: 6; **Exchanges:** 3 Lean Meat, 3 Veg
Per serving: CAL 252 (38% from fat); PRO 24.4g; FAT 10.7g (sat 2.8g); CARB 14.4g; FIB 1.2g; CHOL 81mg; IRON 2.1mg; SOD 397mg; CALC 35mg

Chilled Asparagus With Feta Vinaigrette

This dressing can also be used over salmon or salad greens.

1¼ pounds asparagus
2 tablespoons (½ ounce) crumbled feta cheese
2½ tablespoons lemon juice
1½ tablespoons orange juice
1 tablespoon water
2 teaspoons Dijon mustard
2 teaspoons vegetable oil
2 drops hot sauce
½ cup diced red bell pepper

1. Snap off tough ends of asparagus. Remove scales with a knife or vegetable peeler, if desired. Arrange asparagus spokelike on a 12-inch round glass platter with stem ends toward outside of platter. Cover with heavy-duty plastic wrap, and vent. Microwave at HIGH 4 minutes or until crisp-tender, rotating platter a half-turn after 2 minutes. Let stand, covered, 2 minutes. Cover and chill.

2. Combine feta cheese, juices, water, Dijon mustard, vegetable oil, and hot sauce; stir with a whisk. Divide asparagus evenly among 4 plates, and top each serving with 2 tablespoons feta dressing and 2 tablespoons red bell pepper. Yield: 4 servings.

Points: 1; **Exchanges:** 1 Veg, ½ Fat
Per serving: CAL 62 (51% from fat); PRO 2.7g; FAT 3.5g (sat 1g); CARB 6.6g; FIB 2.1g; CHOL 3mg; IRON 1mg; SOD 120mg; CALC 38mg

Lemon Cream Tart

1 large egg white
2 tablespoons stick margarine
3 tablespoons sugar
3 cups reduced-fat vanilla wafer crumbs (about 36 cookies)
Cooking spray
3 large eggs
1 (14-ounce) can low-fat sweetened condensed milk
1 tablespoon grated lemon rind
½ cup fresh lemon juice
1 cup frozen reduced-calorie whipped topping, thawed and divided

10 lemon rind strips (optional)
Mint leaves (optional)

1. Preheat oven to 325°

2. Combine egg white, margarine, and sugar, and beat at high speed of a mixer until blended. Add vanilla wafer crumbs, and toss with a fork until moist.

3. Press crumb mixture into bottom and up sides of a 9-inch round tart pan coated with cooking spray. Bake at 325° for 15 minutes or until lightly browned. Let cool on a wire rack.

4. Combine eggs, sweetened condensed milk, grated lemon rind, and lemon juice in a medium bowl, stirring with a whisk until blended. Pour mixture into prepared crust. Bake at 325° for 30 minutes or until filling is set. Let cool completely. Top with whipped topping. Garnish tart with lemon rind strips and mint, if desired. Yield: 10 servings (serving size: 1 wedge and 1½ tablespoons whipped topping).

Points: 6; **Exchanges:** 2½ Starch, 1 Fat
Per serving: CAL 256 (27% from fat); PRO 6.5g; FAT 7.8g (sat 2.7g); CARB 41g; FIB 0g; CHOL 71mg; IRON 0.2mg; SOD 159mg; CALC 33mg

---

R O M A N T I C   A N N I V E R S A R Y   D I N N E R

Serves 2

Romaine salad
(1 cup sliced romaine lettuce with 1 tablespoon fat-free dressing per person)

Pesto Lamb Chops

Pasta and Red Peppers

Raspberry-Champagne Sorbet

Pesto Lamb Chops

½ cup fresh basil leaves
1½ teaspoons grated Parmesan cheese
1½ teaspoons pine nuts
1 garlic clove, halved
2 tablespoons plain fat-free yogurt
4 (4-ounce) lean lamb rib chops
Basil sprigs (optional)

**Quick-to-fix Pesto Lamb
Chops and Pasta and
Red Peppers leave plenty
of time for romance.**

1. Place basil, cheese, nuts, and garlic in a food processor bowl; process until smooth. Spoon mixture into a small bowl; stir in yogurt. Cover and chill 30 minutes.

2. Trim fat from chops. Prepare grill or broiler. Place chops on grill rack or broiler pan, and cook 5 minutes. Turn chops; spread basil mixture evenly over chops. Cook 5 minutes or until desired degree of doneness. Garnish with basil sprigs, if desired. Yield: 2 servings.

Points: 5; **Exchanges:** 4 Lean Meat
Per serving: CAL 214 (41% from fat); PRO 27.8g; FAT 9.8g (sat 3.4g); CARB 2.1g; FIB 0.1g; CHOL 84mg; IRON 1.8mg; SOD 108mg; CALC 76mg

Pasta and Red Peppers

Cooking spray
1½ teaspoons reduced-calorie stick margarine

1 medium red bell pepper, cut into strips
¼ cup sliced green onions
1 large garlic clove, minced
⅓ cup fat-free Italian dressing
2 cups hot cooked linguine (about 4 ounces uncooked pasta)

1. Coat a medium nonstick skillet with cooking spray; add margarine, and place over medium-high heat until margarine melts. Add red bell pepper strips, green onions, and garlic; sauté until tender. Stir in Italian dressing, and cook until thoroughly heated, stirring occasionally. Add pasta, and cook just until mixture is thoroughly heated, tossing gently. Yield: 2 servings (serving size: 1 cup).

Points: 6; **Exchanges:** 3½ Starch, ½ Fat
Per serving: CAL 293 (10% from fat); PRO 9.1g; Fat 3.4g (sat 0.9g); CARB 56.2g; FIB 2.6g; CHOL 0mg; IRON 3.3mg; SOD 467mg; CALC 35mg

Raspberry-Champagne Sorbet

This sorbet is so wonderful you'll be pleased to have some in the freezer for later.

6½ cups raspberries
1   cup sugar
1½ cups brut champagne, chilled
½   cup orange juice
Additional raspberries (optional)

1. Place raspberries and sugar in a food processor; process until smooth. Strain raspberry mixture through a sieve into a large bowl; discard seeds. Add champagne and orange juice to raspberry purée; stir well.

2. Pour raspberry mixture into the freezer can of an ice cream freezer; freeze according to manufacturer's instructions (mixture may take longer to freeze due to the alcohol in the champagne). Spoon sorbet into a freezer-safe container; cover and freeze 1 hour or until firm.

3. Scoop sorbet into individual dessert bowls. Garnish with additional raspberries, if desired. Serve immediately. Yield: 12 servings (serving size: ½ cup).

Points: 1; **Exchanges:** 1 Starch, 1 Fruit
Per serving: CAL 126 (3% from fat); PRO 0.8g; FAT 0.4g (sat 0g); CARB 26.2g; FIB 5.3g; CHOL 0mg; IRON 0.6mg; SOD 1mg; CALC 18mg

---

E L E G A N T   D I N N E R   F O R   S I X

Serves 6

Garlic-Sage Cornish Hens
With Wild Rice

Orange-Kissed Brussels Sprouts

Fudgy Soufflé Cake
With Warm Turtle Sauce

Garlic-Sage Cornish Hens
With Wild Rice

Cornish hens are usually found in the frozen meat case of supermarkets.

3   (1-pound) Cornish hens
Cooking spray
2½ teaspoons olive oil
2   teaspoons minced fresh or ½ teaspoon dried sage

¼   teaspoon salt
¼   teaspoon pepper
3   garlic cloves, crushed
3   cups hot cooked wild rice

1. Preheat oven to 350°.

2. Remove and discard giblets and necks from Cornish hens. Rinse hens under cold water, and pat them dry. Remove skin, and trim excess fat. Split each hen in half lengthwise, using kitchen scissors or an electric knife. Place hen halves, meaty sides up, on a broiler pan coated with cooking spray.

3. Combine olive oil, sage, salt, pepper, and garlic; rub evenly over hen halves. Bake at 350° for 1 hour or until done. Serve with wild rice. Yield: 6 servings (serving size: 1 hen half and ½ cup rice).

Points: 6; **Exchanges:** 3½ Very Lean Meat, 1 Starch, 1 Fat
Per serving: CAL 253 (30% from fat); PRO 27.7g; FAT 8.5g (sat 2g); CARB 15.6g; FIB 1.1g; CHOL 76mg; IRON 1.5mg; SOD 173mg; CALC 21mg

Orange-Kissed Brussels Sprouts

When grating orange rind, avoid the pith, the bitter-tasting white layer just beneath the surface.

1½ pounds Brussels sprouts, trimmed and halved
1½ teaspoons grated orange rind
½   cup fresh orange juice
¼   teaspoon salt
⅛   teaspoon pepper

1. Steam Brussels sprouts, covered, 15 minutes or until tender. Drain Brussels sprouts; return to pan. Add orange rind, juice, salt, and pepper; cook over medium heat 2 minutes, stirring constantly. Yield: 6 servings (serving size: ¾ cup).

Points: 0; **Exchanges:** 2 Veg
Per serving: CAL 53 (1% from fat); PRO 3.6g; FAT 0.3g (sat 0.1g); CARB 11.5g; FIB 4.4g; CHOL 0mg; IRON 1.5mg; SOD 123mg; CALC 46mg

Fudgy Soufflé Cake
With Warm Turtle Sauce

No more dashing from oven to table—just bake the soufflé; then serve it warm, at room temperature, or chilled. Once it has fallen, it takes on the consistency of a dense fudge cake.

Butter-flavored cooking spray
¼   teaspoon sugar
½   cup unsweetened cocoa
6   tablespoons hot water
2   tablespoons stick margarine
3   tablespoons all-purpose flour
¾   cup 1% low-fat milk
¼   cup sugar
⅛   teaspoon salt
4   large egg whites (at room temperature)
3   tablespoons sugar
Warm Turtle Sauce

1. Preheat oven to 375°.

2. Coat a 1½-quart soufflé dish with cooking spray; sprinkle with ¼ teaspoon sugar. Set aside.

3. Combine cocoa and hot water in a bowl; stir well, and set aside.

4. Melt margarine in a small, heavy saucepan over medium heat. Add flour; cook 1 minute, stirring constantly with a whisk. Add milk, ¼ cup sugar, and salt; cook 3 minutes or until mixture is thick, stirring constantly. Remove from heat, and stir in cocoa mixture. Spoon into a large bowl, and let cool slightly.

5. Beat egg whites at high speed of a mixer until foamy. Add 3 tablespoons sugar, 1 tablespoon at a time, beating until stiff peaks form. Gently fold 1 cup egg white mixture into cocoa mixture; gently fold in remaining egg white mixture. Spoon into prepared soufflé dish.

6. Bake at 375° for 35 minutes or until puffy and set. Remove from oven; serve warm, at room temperature, or chilled with Warm Turtle Sauce. Yield: 6 servings (serving size: 1 wedge and about 1 tablespoon sauce).

Points: 6; **Exchanges:** 2½ Starch, 1 Fat
Per serving: CAL 251 (28% from fat); PRO 6.1g; FAT 7.8g (sat 1.7g); CARB 39.1g; FIB 0.4g; CHOL 2mg; IRON 1.6mg; SOD 202mg; CALC 62mg

WARM TURTLE SAUCE:
6   tablespoons fat-free caramel-flavored
        sundae syrup
3   tablespoons chopped pecans, toasted

1. Place caramel syrup in a small bowl, and microwave at HIGH 30 seconds or until warm.

Stir in chopped pecans. Yield: ½ cup (serving size: about 1 tablespoon).

Points: 2; **Exchanges:** 1 Starch, ½ Fat
Per serving: CAL 89 (25% from fat); PRO 0.3g; FAT 2.5g (sat 0.2g); CARB 16.2g; FIB 0.3g; CHOL 0mg; IRON 0.1mg; SOD 55mg; CALC 9mg

---

PROMOTION CELEBRATION

Serves 4

Shrimp Kedgeree

Green salad
(1 cup salad greens and 1 tablespoon
fat-free salad dressing per person)

Cornmeal-Raisin Scones

Grand Marnier Soufflés

Shrimp Kedgeree

1   hard-cooked large egg
1⅓ cups low-salt chicken broth
½   cup uncooked long-grain rice
½   cup cooked peeled chopped shrimp
        (about 6 ounces)
1   tablespoon minced fresh chives
¼   teaspoon salt
¼   teaspoon paprika
⅛   teaspoon coarsely ground pepper
Dash of ground nutmeg
1   tablespoon chopped fresh parsley
8   watercress sprigs (optional)
Additional cooked peeled shrimp (optional)

1. Slice egg in half lengthwise, and remove yolk. Finely chop egg white, and press yolk through a sieve, using the back of a spoon. Set aside.

2. Bring broth to a boil in a medium saucepan. Add rice; cover, reduce heat, and simmer 20 minutes or until liquid is absorbed.

3. Combine cooked rice, chopped egg white, shrimp, and next 5 ingredients; toss gently. Spoon 1 cup rice mixture onto each of 2 plates; top with egg yolk and parsley. Garnish with watercress and additional shrimp, if desired. Yield: 2 servings.

Points: 6; **Exchanges:** 2½ Starch, 2½ Very Lean Meat
Per serving: CAL 304 (15% from fat); PRO 23.7g; FAT 4.9g (sat 1.4g); CARB 39.3g; FIB 0.7g; CHOL 251mg; IRON 5.6mg; SOD 546mg; CALC 61mg

Fudgy Soufflé Cake With
Warm Turtle Sauce

Enjoy the East Indian and English flavors of Shrimp Kedgeree and Cornmeal-Raisin Scones.

Cornmeal-Raisin Scones

⅔ cup all-purpose flour
¼ cup yellow cornmeal
3 tablespoons sugar
1 teaspoon baking powder
¼ teaspoon baking soda
⅛ teaspoon salt
1 tablespoon chilled stick margarine, cut into small pieces
2 tablespoons golden raisins
⅓ cup low-fat buttermilk
1 large egg, lightly beaten
Cooking spray

1. Preheat oven to 375°.

2. Combine all-purpose flour, cornmeal, sugar, baking powder, baking soda, and salt in a bowl; cut in margarine with a pastry blender or 2 knives until mixture resembles fine meal. Add golden raisins, and toss well. Combine low-fat buttermilk and beaten egg, and add to dry ingredients, stirring just until moist (dough will be sticky).

3. Spoon dough evenly into 5 mounds on a baking sheet coated with cooking spray. Bake at 375° for 18 minutes or until golden. Serve warm. Yield: 5 scones (serving size: 1 scone).

Note: Store remaining scones in an airtight container at room temperature up to 2 days.

Points: 4; Exchanges: 2 Starch, ½ Fat
Per serving: CAL 171 (21% from fat); PRO 4.3g; FAT 4g (sat 0.8g); CARB 29.7g; FIB 1g; CHOL 44mg; IRON 1.4mg; SOD 171mg; CALC 85mg

Grand Marnier Soufflés

Cooking spray
2 tablespoons sugar, divided
1 tablespoon skim milk
1 teaspoon all-purpose flour
2 teaspoons Grand Marnier (orange-flavored liqueur)
1 large egg, separated

½ teaspoon powdered sugar
⅛ teaspoon cream of tartar
Chocolate Sauce

1. Preheat oven to 375°.

2. Coat 2 (8-ounce) soufflé dishes or custard cups with cooking spray. Sprinkle dishes evenly with 1 tablespoon sugar, carefully shaking to coat bottom and sides of each dish; set aside.

3. Combine remaining 1 tablespoon sugar, milk, and flour in a small microwave-safe bowl; stir with a whisk until blended. Microwave at HIGH 20 seconds or until thick and bubbly; stir well. Stir in liqueur; set aside.

4. Place egg yolk in a medium bowl; beat at medium speed of a mixer until thick and pale. Add milk mixture; beat well. Set aside.

5. Place egg white, powdered sugar, and cream of tartar in a bowl; beat at high speed of an electric mixer until stiff peaks form. Gently fold egg white mixture into milk mixture. Spoon evenly into prepared dishes. Bake at 375° for 15 minutes or until soufflés are puffed. Spoon 2½ tablespoons Chocolate Sauce over each soufflé. Serve immediately. Yield: 2 servings.

Points: 4; Exchanges: 2 Starch, ½ Fat
Per serving: CAL 169 (18% from fat); PRO 4.4g; FAT 3.3g (sat 1g); CARB 30.9g; FIB 0g; CHOL 111mg; IRON 0.9mg; SOD 39mg; CALC 26mg

CHOCOLATE SAUCE:
¼ cup water
1½ tablespoons sugar
1 tablespoon unsweetened cocoa
½ teaspoon cornstarch
2 teaspoons Grand Marnier (orange-flavored liqueur)

1. Combine first 4 ingredients in a small saucepan, stirring with a whisk until smooth. Place over medium heat, and cook until mixture is thick and bubbly, stirring constantly. Add liqueur; cook 1 minute, stirring constantly. Remove from heat; let cool. Yield: 5 tablespoons.

Points: 0; Exchanges: ¼ Starch
Per serving: CAL 24 (8% from fat); PRO 0.3g; FAT 0.1g (sat 0.1g); CARB 5.5g; FIB 0g; CHOL 0mg; IRON 0.5mg; SOD 1mg; CALC 4mg

---

THEY SAY IT'S YOUR BIRTHDAY

Serves 4

Filet Mignon With
Mushroom-Wine Sauce

Long-grain white rice
(1 cup per person)

Steamed broccoli spears
(1 cup per person)

Dinner rolls (1 per person)

Marbled Cheesecake

Filet Mignon With Mushroom-Wine Sauce

Shiitake mushrooms lend a full-bodied, beefy taste to the sauce. However, white or crimini mushrooms can be substituted, resulting in a milder tasting sauce.

1 tablespoon stick margarine, divided
Cooking spray
⅓ cup finely chopped shallot
½ pound fresh shiitake mushrooms, stems removed
1½ cups Cabernet Sauvignon or other dry red wine, divided
1 (10½-ounce) can beef consommé, undiluted and divided
Cracked pepper
4 (4-ounce) filet mignon steaks (about 1 inch thick)
1 tablespoon low-sodium soy sauce
2 teaspoons cornstarch
1 teaspoon dried thyme
Thyme sprigs (optional)

1. Melt 1½ teaspoons margarine in a nonstick skillet coated with cooking spray over medium heat. Add shallot and mushrooms; sauté 4 minutes. Add 1 cup wine and ¾ cup consommé; cook 5 minutes, stirring frequently. Remove mushrooms with a slotted spoon, and place in a bowl. Increase heat to high; cook wine mixture 5 minutes or until reduced to ½ cup. Add to mushrooms in bowl; set aside. Wipe skillet dry with a paper towel.

2. Sprinkle pepper over steaks. Melt remaining

The elegance and ease of Filet Mignon With Mushroom-Wine Sauce make it ideal for entertaining.

1½ teaspoons margarine in skillet coated with cooking spray over medium heat. Add steaks, and cook 3 minutes on each side or until browned. Reduce heat to medium-low; cook 1½ minutes on each side or until done. Place on a platter, and keep warm.

3. Combine soy sauce and cornstarch, and stir well. Add remaining wine and consommé to skillet; scrape skillet with a wooden spoon to loosen browned bits. Bring to a boil, and cook 1 minute. Add mushroom mixture, cornstarch mixture, and dried thyme; bring to a boil, and cook 1 minute, stirring constantly. Serve with steaks. Garnish with thyme sprigs, if desired. Yield: 4 servings (serving size: 3 ounces meat and ½ cup sauce).

Points: 6; **Exchanges:** 3½ Lean Meat, ½ Starch, ½ Fat
Per serving: CAL 250 (39% from fat); PRO 28.5g; FAT 10.7g (sat 3.6g); CARB 9.4g; FIB 0.9g; CHOL 84mg; IRON 5.1mg; SOD 712mg; CALC 30mg

Marbled Cheesecake

This sensational cheesecake, made with fat-free cream cheese and sour cream, can be whipped up in no time flat.

Cooking spray
½   cup chocolate wafer cookie crumbs
      (about 8 cookies)
1   cup sugar
¼   cup all-purpose flour
1   tablespoon vanilla extract
2   (8-ounce) tubs fat-free cream cheese,
      softened
1   (16-ounce) carton fat-free sour cream
4   large eggs
3   (1-ounce) squares sweet baking chocolate,
      melted

1. Coat a 9-inch springform pan with cooking spray; sprinkle with chocolate wafer cookie crumbs, and set aside.

2. Preheat oven to 325°.

3. Combine sugar and next 4 ingredients in a food processor; process just until smooth. Add eggs; process 5 seconds or just until blended (overprocessing will incorporate air, which will make the baked cheesecake crack).

4. Pour half of cheese mixture into a bowl; add melted chocolate, stirring until well blended. Spoon alternating mounds of plain and chocolate cheese mixtures into prepared pan; swirl with a knife to create a marbled effect. Bake at 325° for 1 hour or until almost set. Turn off oven, and partially open oven door; leave cheesecake in oven 1 hour. Remove cheesecake from oven; let cool completely on a wire rack. Cover and chill 8 hours. Yield: 12 servings (serving size: 1 wedge).

Note: Cover remaining cheesecake with plastic wrap, and store in refrigerator up to 5 days.

Points: 5; Exchanges: 2 Starch, ½ Lean Meat, ½ Fat
Per serving: CAL 218 (20% from fat); PRO 11.2g; FAT 4.8g (sat 2g); CARB 29.5g; FIB 0.1g; CHOL 85mg; IRON 0.5mg; SOD 295mg; CALC 134mg

MINI CLAMBAKE

Serves 4

Mini Clambake
Red-and-Green Coleslaw
Beer Bread

Mini Clambake

4 ears corn with husks
4 cups water
1 tablespoon salt
8 small red potatoes
2 (1½-pound) live Maine lobsters
16 small clams in shells, scrubbed
¼ cup margarine, cut into small pieces
Lemon wedges

1. Remove husks from corn, and set husks aside. Scrub silks from corn, and set corn aside.

2. Combine water, salt, and potatoes in a 19-quart stockpot; bring to a boil. Add lobsters, and cover and cook 12 minutes. Remove lobsters from pot, and set aside. Add clams to pot, and cover and cook 10 minutes or until shells open.

Remove clams from pot, and set aside; discard any unopened shells.

3. Add corn to pot; cover and cook 5 minutes. Remove corn and potatoes from pot, and set aside. Reserve 1 cup cooking liquid.

4. Combine the reserved cooking liquid and margarine in a blender, and process until margarine melts.

5. Arrange the cornhusks spokelike on a large serving platter. Arrange the lobsters, clams, corn, and red potatoes on top of the cornhusks. Serve with warm margarine mixture and lemon wedges. Yield: 4 servings (serving size: ½ lobster, 4 clams, 1 ear corn, 2 potatoes, and 6 tablespoons sauce).

Points: 9; Exchanges: 1½ Very Lean Meat, 4½ Starch, 2 Fat
Per serving: CAL 488 (24% from fat); PRO 25.2g; FAT 13.2g (sat 2.6g); CARB 73.2g; FIB 8.3g; CHOL 54mg; IRON 6.1mg; SOD 882 mg; CALC 110mg

Red-and-Green Coleslaw

⅓ cup light mayonnaise
⅓ cup fat-free sour cream
¼ cup chopped fresh parsley
1 tablespoon sugar
2 teaspoons lemon juice
½ teaspoon salt
¼ teaspoon ground ginger
6 cups thinly sliced green cabbage
2 cups thinly sliced red cabbage
½ cup thinly sliced celery

1. Combine first 7 ingredients in a large bowl; stir with a whisk until blended. Add green and red cabbage and celery; toss to coat. Cover and chill. Yield: 4 servings (serving size: 1½ cups).

Points: 2; Exchanges: ½ Starch, 1 Fat, 1 Veg
Per serving: CAL 117 (34% from fat); PRO 3.3g; FAT 4.4g (sat 3.6g); CARB 17.1g; FIB 3.6g; CHOL 0mg; IRON 1.1mg; SOD 555mg; CALC 80mg

Beer Bread

Serve leftover slices of this bread toasted at another meal.

Cooking spray
2 teaspoons self-rising flour
3 cups self-rising flour

STUFF IT

Manicotti may be fluted or smooth, straight or angled but all do the same job: hold cheesy fillings.

1 Prepare dish
Spread 1 cup pasta sauce in a baking dish before adding the stuffed manicotti.

2 Stuff shells
Using a teaspoon, carefully stuff the cooked manicotti shells with the cheese mixture.

3 Top with cheese
Sprinkle mozzarella and grated Parmesan cheeses over shells and sauce before baking.

---

3 tablespoons sugar
3 tablespoons reduced-calorie stick margarine, melted
1 (12-ounce) can light beer

1. Preheat oven to 350°.

2. Coat a 9- x 5-inch loaf pan with cooking spray, and lightly dust with 2 teaspoons flour; set aside.

3. Combine 3 cups self-rising flour and sugar in a bowl; stir well, and make a well in center of mixture. Add melted margarine and light beer, stirring just until moist.

4. Pour batter into prepared pan. Bake at 350° for 40 minutes or until a wooden pick inserted in center comes out clean. Let cool in pan 5 minutes on a wire rack. Remove bread from pan, and let cool completely on wire rack. Cut bread into 8 slices, and cut each slice in half. Yield: 16 servings.

Note: Tightly wrap leftover bread, and store in refrigerator up to 5 days.

Points: 2; **Exchanges:** 1½ Starch
Per serving: CAL 107 (11% from fat); PRO 2.4g; FAT 1.3g (sat 0.2g); CARB 20.9g; FIB 0.8g; CHOL 0mg; IRON 1.1mg; SOD 332mg; CALC 83mg

GRADUATION GATHERING

Serves 6

Four-Cheese Manicotti

Mixed green salad
(1 cup torn mixed salad greens with 1 tablespoon fat-free Italian dressing per person)

Herbed Breadsticks

Banana Split Ice Cream

Four-Cheese Manicotti

If you don't have individual casserole dishes, use a 13- x 9-inch baking dish to prepare this entrée.

12 uncooked manicotti
Cooking spray
½ cup finely chopped onion
3 garlic cloves, minced
1 cup (4 ounces) shredded part-skim mozzarella cheese, divided

½ cup (2 ounces) grated fresh Parmesan cheese, divided
1 teaspoon dried Italian seasoning
½ teaspoon pepper
1 (15-ounce) carton fat-free ricotta cheese
1 (6-ounce) package garden vegetable-flavored light cream cheese, softened
4 ounces block fat-free cream cheese (about ½ cup), softened
½ (10-ounce) package frozen chopped spinach, thawed, drained, and squeezed dry
1 (27.5-ounce) jar reduced-fat, reduced sodium tomato-and-herb pasta sauce
Oregano sprigs (optional)

1. Preheat oven to 350°.

2. Cook pasta according to package directions, omitting salt and fat; set aside.

3. Coat a small nonstick skillet with cooking spray, and place over medium-high heat until hot. Add onion and garlic; sauté 3 minutes. Remove from heat; set aside.

4. Combine ½ cup mozzarella cheese, ¼ cup Parmesan cheese, Italian seasoning, pepper, ricotta cheese, and softened cream cheeses in a bowl; beat at medium speed of a mixer until smooth. Stir in onion mixture and spinach. Spoon cheese mixture into cooked manicotti (about ⅓ cup per shell).

5. Divide 1 cup pasta sauce evenly between 6 individual casserole dishes coated with cooking spray. Arrange 2 stuffed manicotti in each dish. Pour remaining sauce over each serving. Place dishes on a baking sheet. Cover each dish with foil, and bake at 350° for 25 minutes. Sprinkle with remaining mozzarella and Parmesan cheeses; bake, uncovered, an additional 5 minutes. Garnish with oregano, if desired. Yield: 6 servings (serving size: 2 manicotti).

Points: 8; **Exchanges:** 3 Lean Meat, 2 Starch, 2 Veg
Per serving: CAL 386 (27% from fat); PRO 30g; FAT 11.7g (sat 6.9g); CARB 41.5g; FIB 4.3g; CHOL 49mg; IRON 0.9mg; SOD 1,012mg; CALC 495mg

Herbed Breadsticks

1 (8-ounce) loaf French bread
1 tablespoon olive oil

1 garlic clove, halved
¾ teaspoon dried oregano
¾ teaspoon dried basil
⅛ teaspoon salt

1. Preheat oven to 300°.

2. Cut French bread in half crosswise, and cut each piece in half horizontally. Brush olive oil evenly over cut sides of bread, and rub with garlic. Sprinkle dried oregano, basil, and salt over bread. Cut each piece of bread lengthwise into 3 sticks. Place breadsticks on a baking sheet, and bake at 300° for 25 minutes or until crisp. Serve warm. Yield: 1 dozen (serving size: 2 breadsticks).

Points: 3; **Exchanges:** 1½ Starch, ½ Fat
Per serving: CAL 149 (22% from fat); PRO 4.1g; FAT 3.6g (sat 0.6g); CARB 24.7g; FIB 0.7g; CHOL 2mg; IRON 1.1mg; SOD 304mg; CALC 26mg

Banana Split Ice Cream

5 cups 1% low-fat milk, divided
4 large egg yolks
2 (14-ounce) cans fat-free sweetened condensed skim milk
2 cups mashed ripe banana
2 tablespoons fresh lime juice
2 tablespoons vanilla extract
¾ cup fat-free double chocolate sundae syrup
½ cup chopped pecans, toasted
⅓ cup maraschino cherries, quartered

1. Combine 2½ cups 1% low-fat milk and egg yolks in a heavy saucepan, and stir mixture well with a whisk. Cook over medium heat 10 minutes or until mixture thickens and coats a spoon, stirring constantly (do not boil). Combine egg yolk mixture, remaining 2½ cups 1% low-fat milk, and sweetened condensed skim milk in a

Using a bottled pasta sauce shortens the prep time for this hearty Four-Cheese Manicotti.

large bowl; stir well. Cover and chill completely.

2. Add mashed banana, lime juice, and vanilla extract to milk mixture, and stir well. Pour mixture into the freezer can of an ice cream freezer, and freeze according to manufacturer's instructions. Spoon ice cream into a large freezer-safe container, and fold in chocolate syrup, chopped pecans, and maraschino cherries. Cover and freeze 2 hours or until firm. Yield: 24 servings (serving size: ½ cup).

Points: 4; **Exchanges:** 2 Starch, ½ Fat
Per serving: CAL 189 (15% from fat); PRO 5.3g; FAT 3.2g (sat 0.8g); CARB 34.3g; FIB 0.7g; CHOL 40mg; IRON 0.2mg; SOD 67mg; CALC 136mg

FIRESIDE SUPPER FOR TWO

Serves 2

Cassoulet

Curly Endive-and-Grape Salad

French rolls (1 each)

Ginger Brûlée

Cassoulet

This stew was named for the earthenware casserole it was often cooked in. Our version has the traditional navy beans, lamb, and tomatoes, but it doesn't take the traditional three days to make!

Banana Split Ice Cream is chock-full of bananas, cherries, chocolate, and nuts.

¼ pound lean boned leg of lamb
Cooking spray
⅔ cup thinly sliced carrot
½ cup thinly sliced leek
½ cup chopped onion
2 turkey-bacon slices, chopped
2 garlic cloves, minced
⅔ cup drained canned navy beans
½ cup dry red wine
¼ teaspoon dried thyme
⅛ teaspoon pepper
1 bay leaf
1 (14-ounce) can no-salt-added whole
   tomatoes, undrained and chopped
¼ cup dry breadcrumbs
2 tablespoons chopped fresh parsley
1 garlic clove, minced

1. Trim fat from lamb; cut lamb into ¾-inch cubes, and set aside.

2. Coat a large nonstick skillet with cooking spray, and place over medium heat until hot. Add carrot and next 4 ingredients; cover and cook 5 minutes, stirring occasionally. Add lamb; cook, uncovered, 3 minutes or until browned, stirring occasionally. Add beans and next 5 ingredients; stir well. Bring to a boil over medium-high heat, and cook, uncovered, 8 minutes, stirring occasionally. Discard bay leaf.

3. Preheat oven to 350°.

4. Combine breadcrumbs, parsley, and 1 garlic clove; stir well, and set aside.

5. Spoon lamb mixture into 2 (2-cup) individual casserole dishes coated with cooking spray; top with breadcrumb mixture. Bake at 350° for 15 minutes. Yield: 2 servings (serving size 1½ cups).

Points: 7; **Exchanges:** 2 Med-fat Meat, 2½ Starch, 2 Veg
Per serving: CAL 385 (18% from fat); PRO 25.3g; FAT 7.7g (sat 2g); CARB 44.9g; FIB 5.3g; CHOL 54mg; IRON 5.6mg; SOD 699mg; CALC 187mg

Curly Endive-and-Grape Salad

1 tablespoon red wine vinegar
2 teaspoons water
1 teaspoon honey
½ teaspoon extra-virgin olive oil
¼ teaspoon Dijon mustard
⅛ teaspoon salt
⅛ teaspoon pepper
2 cups torn curly endive
½ cup seedless red grapes, halved
4 teaspoons crumbled blue cheese

1. Combine first 7 ingredients in a bowl; stir well with a whisk. Combine endive and grapes in a bowl. Add vinegar mixture; toss to coat. Sprinkle with cheese. Yield: 2 servings (serving size: 1 cup).

Points: 2; **Exchanges:** 2 Veg, ½ Fat
Per serving: CAL 71 (43% from fat); PRO 2.3g; FAT 3.4g (sat 1.5g); CARB 9.1g; FIB 0.6g; CHOL 5mg; IRON 0.6mg; SOD 270mg; CALC 68mg

Ginger Brûlée

5 tablespoons water
1 tablespoon peeled minced fresh ginger
1 tablespoon sugar
¾ cup skim milk
½ cup egg substitute
¼ cup sugar
2 tablespoons instant nonfat dry milk powder
1 teaspoon vanilla extract
Cooking spray
1 teaspoon brown sugar

1. Preheat oven to 325°.

2. Combine first 3 ingredients in a small saucepan. Bring to a boil; reduce heat, and simmer, uncovered, 5 minutes or until mixture is reduced by half. Remove from heat; strain mixture, reserving liquid. Discard ginger.

3. Combine ginger liquid, skim milk, and next 4 ingredients in a small bowl; beat at medium speed of a mixer until blended. Divide mixture evenly between 2 (8-ounce) ramekins coated with cooking spray. Place ramekins in an 8-inch square baking pan. Add hot water to pan to depth of 1 inch. Bake at 325° for 55 minutes or until set. Remove ramekins from water; let cool 15 minutes. Cover and chill.

4. Sprinkle brown sugar evenly over top of each custard. Place ramekins on a baking sheet. Broil 1 minute or until sugar melts. Serve immediately. Yield: 2 servings.

Points: 5; **Exchanges** 2 Starch, 1 Sk Milk
Per serving: CAL 225 (2% from fat); PRO 11.8g; FAT 0.4g (sat 0.1g); CARB 42.8g; CHOL 3mg; IRON 1.2mg; SOD 179 mg; CALC 229mg

When Time Is of The Essence

SIMPLIFY MEALTIME WITH THESE
GREAT MAKE-AHEAD MENUS,
THE ULTIMATE CULINARY SHORTCUT.

Many people are searching for simplicity, and for good reason. The simplest things—whether fashion, furniture, or especially food—are often the most tasteful. On the flip side, there seems to be a correlation between a food's prep time and the calories and fat it contains: The more convenient a food—think Big Macs and frozen pot pies—the more fattening. But not every culinary shortcut is a recipe for diet disaster.

Simplify mealtime without sacrificing nutrition by making meals ahead of time. You tote mouthwatering casseroles to friends who've just had a baby or to the folks moving in next door assuming they don't have time to cook, but you rarely do yourself the same favor. All you need is a little forethought—and the following recipes. Assemble the Spinach Lasagna on Sunday and bake it on Monday for a fuss-free dinner, or let the Mushroom-Stuffed Beef Tenderloin marinate while you're at work so you can invite co-workers for an elegant dinner that takes only 45 minutes to make. After all, it's easier to impress them with a home-cooked meal than an overhead presentation of last quarter's profit-and-loss statement.

Vegetables, olives, and cheese fill the layers of Spinach Lasagna.

PASTA NIGHT

Serves 6

Spinach Lasagna

Thin crispy breadsticks

(2 breadsticks per person)

Caesar Salad

Strawberry Frozen Yogurt

Spinach Lasagna

Cooking spray
2 cups sliced mushrooms
1 cup shredded carrot
1 cup chopped onion
2 (8-ounce) cans no-salt-added tomato sauce
1 (6-ounce) can no-salt-added tomato paste
1 (2¼-ounce) can sliced ripe olives, drained
1½ teaspoons dried oregano
1 teaspoon dried basil
½ teaspoon pepper
1 (10-ounce) package frozen chopped spinach, thawed, drained, and squeezed dry
1½ cups 1% low-fat cottage cheese
3 ounces block fat-free cream cheese (about 6 tablespoons), softened
1 tablespoon lemon juice
9 cooked lasagna noodles
1½ cups (6 ounces) shredded part-skim mozzarella cheese
¼ cup grated Parmesan cheese

1. Coat a large nonstick skillet with cooking spray; place over medium-high heat until hot. Add mushrooms, carrot, and onion; sauté 5 minutes. Remove from heat; stir in tomato sauce and next 5 ingredients. Set aside.

2. Combine spinach and next 3 ingredients in a bowl; stir well, and set aside.

3. Arrange 3 lasagna noodles in bottom of an 11- x 7-inch baking dish coated with cooking spray. Spoon one-third of spinach mixture over noodles. Spoon one-third of mushroom mixture over spinach mixture. Top with one-third of mozzarella cheese. Repeat layers twice with remaining noodles, spinach mixture, mushroom mixture, and mozzarella cheese. Top with Parmesan cheese. (**Make-Ahead Tip:** Cover and chill 8 to 24 hours. Remove lasagna from refrigerator; let stand at room temperature 30 minutes.)

4. Preheat oven to 325°.

5. Uncover lasagna; bake at 325° for 45 minutes or until thoroughly heated. Yield: 6 servings.

Points: 7; **Exchanges:** 2 Med-Fat Meat, 3 Starch, 2 Veg
Per serving: CAL 379 (20% from fat); PRO 27g; FAT 8.3g (sat 4.2g); CHOL 25mg; FIB 6.2g; CARB 50g; IRON 4.1mg; SOD 705mg; CALC 414mg

Caesar Salad

3 (1-ounce) slices white bread
Olive oil-flavored cooking spray

USE YOUR NOODLE

1. Cook lasagna noodles according to the package directions, omitting salt and fat. Drain in a colander and rinse under running water to remove excess starch and prevent sticking. Place noodles in a single layer on the work surface until ready to use.

2. Layer the noodles, spinach mixture, mushroom mixture, and cheese in an 11- x 7-inch baking dish coated with cooking spray. Depending on the brand of noodles, they may need to be trimmed to fit the length of the dish. Fill in with trimmed pieces.

¾   teaspoon garlic powder
½   cup no-salt-added chicken broth
4½ tablespoons fresh lemon juice
1   tablespoon low-sodium Worcestershire
    sauce
1½ teaspoons anchovy paste
½   teaspoon dry mustard
2   garlic cloves, halved
6   cups sliced romaine lettuce
¾   teaspoon cracked pepper
¼   cup (1 ounce) grated fresh Parmesan cheese

1. Preheat oven to 300°.

2. Coat one side of each bread slice with cooking spray; sprinkle evenly with garlic powder. Place bread, coated side up, on a baking sheet. Bake at 300° for 18 minutes or until golden. Cut bread into cubes. (**Make-Ahead Tip:** Store bread cubes in a loosely covered container at room temperature 8 to 24 hours.) Combine chicken broth and next 4 ingredients in a small bowl; stir with a whisk until blended. (**Make-Ahead Tip:** Cover and chill 8 to 24 hours. Stir well before serving.)

3. Rub inside of a large salad bowl with cut sides of garlic; discard garlic. Place lettuce in bowl. Drizzle broth mixture over lettuce, and sprinkle with pepper; toss well. Sprinkle salad with Parmesan cheese, and top with bread cubes. Serve immediately. Yield: 6 servings (serving size: 1 cup).

Points: 2; **Exchanges:** ½ Starch, 1 Veg
Per serving: CAL 80 (26% from fat); PRO 4.5g; FAT 2.3g (sat 0.9g); CARB 10.6g; FIB 1.3g; CHOL 4mg; IRON 1.1mg; SOD 345mg; CALC 89mg

Strawberry Frozen Yogurt

2   cups fresh strawberries, hulled
¾   cup sugar
½   teaspoon grated lemon rind
1¼ cups plain fat-free yogurt
¼   cup skim milk

1. Combine first 3 ingredients in a blender or food processor; process until smooth. Add yogurt and milk; process 30 seconds. Pour into freezer can of an ice cream freezer; freeze according to manufacturer's instructions. Spoon yogurt mixture into a freezer-safe container; cover and freeze 1 hour or until firm. Yield: 4 cups (serving size: ⅔ cup).

Points: 3; **Exchanges:** 1 Starch, 1 Fruit
Per serving: CAL 141 (2% from fat); PRO 3.4g; FAT 0.3g (sat 0.1g); CARB 32.5g; FIB 1.3g; CHOL 1mg; IRON 0.2mg; SOD 42mg; CALC 114mg

SIMPLE SALAD SUPPER

Serves 5

Greek Shrimp Salad

Whole-wheat pita bread

(1 per person)

Ruby Red Grapefruit Sorbet

Greek Shrimp Salad

2   pounds medium shrimp, peeled and
    deveined
2¾ cups cooked orzo (about 1½ cups
    uncooked rice-shaped pasta)
¾   cup chopped green onions
¾   cup (3 ounces) crumbled feta cheese with
    peppercorns
3   tablespoons minced fresh dill
3   tablespoons lemon juice
1   tablespoon olive oil
¼   teaspoon salt
1   cup cherry tomatoes, halved
¾   cup peeled chopped cucumber
15 curly lettuce leaves

1. Bring 6 cups water to a boil in a Dutch oven. Add shrimp; cook 3 minutes or until done. Drain and rinse under cold water. Peel shrimp.

2. Combine shrimp, orzo, and next 3 ingredients in a large bowl. Combine lemon juice, oil, and salt in a bowl; stir well with a whisk. Drizzle over shrimp mixture; toss gently to coat. (**Make-Ahead Tip:** Cover and chill at least 8 hours.)

3. Add cucumber and tomatoes to salad just before serving; toss well. Serve on lettuce-lined plates. Yield: 5 servings (serving size: 1½ cups).

Points: 6; **Exchanges:** 3 Lean Meat, 1½ Starch, 1 Veg
Per serving: CAL 311 (24% from fat); PRO 27.2g; FAT 8.2g (sat 3.3g) CARB 32.2g; FIB 2.1mg; CHOL 192mg; IRON 6.1mg; SOD 526mg; CALC 193mg

Ruby Red Grapefruit Sorbet

1   cup sugar
1   cup water
Dash of salt
1   tablespoon grated Ruby Red grapefruit
     rind
3   cups fresh Ruby Red grapefruit juice
1   cup semisweet sparkling wine

1. Combine sugar, water, and dash of salt in a medium saucepan; stir well. Bring to a boil, and cook 1 minute or until sugar dissolves, stirring constantly. Remove from heat; pour into a large bowl, and stir in grated grapefruit rind. Let mixture cool to room temperature. Stir in Ruby Red grapefruit juice and semisweet sparkling wine.

2. Pour mixture into freezer can of an ice cream freezer, and freeze according to manufacturer's directions. Spoon sorbet into a freezer-safe container; cover and freeze at least 2 hours. Yield: 11 servings (serving size: ½ cup).

Note: Store remaining sorbet in the freezer up to 1 week.

Points: 2; **Exchanges:** ½ Fruit, 1 Starch
Per serving: CAL 122 (0% from fat); PRO 0.4g; FAT 0.1g (sat 0g); CARB 25.2g; FIB 0g; CHOL 0mg; IRON 1.4mg; SOD 16mg; CALC 7mg

---

ELEGANT-BUT-EASY DINNER

Serves 8

Mushroom-Stuffed Beef Tenderloin

Lemon-Basil Carrot Bundles

Whole-wheat dinner rolls
(1 per person)

Charlotte Russe Parfaits

Mushroom-Stuffed Beef Tenderloin

Cooking spray
¾   pound mushrooms, sliced
¾   pound chopped fresh spinach
1½   cups chopped green onions
¼   cup chopped fresh parsley
½   teaspoon salt

1   (4-pound) trimmed beef tenderloin
1   teaspoon salt-free herb-and-spice
     blend
½   cup low-sodium soy sauce
⅓   cup dry sherry
2   tablespoons brown sugar
2   tablespoons honey
2   garlic cloves, minced

1. Coat a large nonstick skillet with cooking spray, and place over medium-high heat until hot. Add mushrooms, spinach, and green onions; sauté 3 minutes or until tender. Remove skillet from heat, and stir in parsley and salt. Set mixture aside.

2. Trim fat from tenderloin. To butterfly, slice tenderloin lengthwise, cutting to, but not through, other side, leaving one long side connected; open flat. Sprinkle herb-and-spice blend over inside of tenderloin. Spread mushroom mixture down center of tenderloin to within ½ inch of sides. Fold sides of tenderloin over mushroom mixture; secure at 2-inch intervals with heavy string. Set aside.

3. Combine soy sauce, sherry, brown sugar, honey, and garlic in a large shallow baking dish; stir mixture well. Add tenderloin, turning to coat. Cover and marinate in refrigerator 8 hours, turning occasionally.

4. Preheat oven to 425°.

5. Remove tenderloin from shallow baking dish, reserving marinade. Place tenderloin on a broiler pan coated with cooking spray. Insert meat thermometer into thickest portion of the tenderloin. Bake at 425° for 45 minutes or until meat thermometer registers 135° (rare) or 160° (medium), basting occasionally with the reserved marinade.

6. Place tenderloin on a large serving platter, and let stand 10 minutes before slicing. Yield: 16 servings.

Points: 4; **Exchanges:** 3 Lean Meat, 1 Veg
Per serving: CAL 178 (34% from fat); PRO 21.3g; FAT 6.8g (sat 2.6g); CARB 6.7g; FIB 1.4g; CHOL 60mg; IRON 3.7mg; SOD 333mg; CALC 38mg

Lemon-Basil Carrot Bundles

6   medium carrots, cut into 3-inch julienne
     strips
½   cup water
2   tablespoons lemon juice
2   teaspoons sugar
2   garlic cloves, minced
1   tablespoon minced fresh or 1 teaspoon
     dried basil
1   tablespoon olive oil
½   teaspoon grated lemon rind
2   green onions

1. Combine first 5 ingredients in a medium saucepan; bring to a boil over medium heat. Cover, reduce heat, and simmer 8 minutes or until carrot strips are crisp-tender. Drain carrot strips, reserving cooking liquid. Set carrot strips aside. Add basil, lemon rind, and olive oil to cooking liquid; stir well, and set mixture aside.

2. Trim white portion from green onions; reserve for another use. Place green onion tops in a small bowl, and cover with boiling water. Drain immediately. Rinse under cold water; drain well. Cut green onion tops into 8 thin strips.

3. Divide carrot strips into 8 equal bundles; tie each bundle with a green onion strip. Place bundles in a shallow dish; pour basil mixture over bundles. Cover and chill at least 2 hours.

4. Remove bundles from basil mixture using a slotted spoon; discard basil mixture. Arrange bundles on a serving platter. Yield: 8 servings.

Points: 0; **Exchanges:** 1 Veg
Per serving: CAL 28 (19% from fat); PRO 0.5g; FAT 0.6g (sat 0.1g); CARB 5.7g; FIB 1.3g; CHOL 0mg; IRON 0.3mg; SOD 14mg; CALC 14mg

This Charlotte Russe Parfait is a simplified version of the more elaborate Russian classic.

Charlotte Russe Parfaits

½ cup sugar
¼ cup cornstarch
1 large egg
2½ cups skim milk
2 tablespoons margarine
1 teaspoon vanilla extract
1½ cups frozen reduced-calorie whipped topping, thawed and divided
20 ladyfingers
3 tablespoons black cherry preserves with Chambord liqueur or red currant jelly
Mint leaves (optional)

1. Combine sugar, cornstarch, and egg in a large bowl; stir well with a whisk, and set mixture aside.

2. Heat milk over medium-high heat in a medium saucepan to 180° or until tiny bubbles form around edge (do not boil). Gradually add hot milk to sugar mixture, stirring constantly with whisk. Return milk mixture to saucepan. Add margarine, and cook over medium heat 5 minutes or until thick and bubbly, stirring constantly. Reduce heat to low, and cook an additional 2 minutes, stirring constantly. Remove saucepan from heat, and stir in vanilla extract. Pour mixture into a large bowl; cover surface with plastic wrap, and let cool completely. Uncover and gently fold in 1 cup whipped topping; cover and chill at least 2 hours.

3. Split ladyfingers in half lengthwise. Line each of 8 dessert compotes with 5 ladyfinger halves, standing upright. Spoon ½ cup custard into center of each compote. Place preserves in a small microwave-safe bowl, and microwave at HIGH 30 seconds or until preserves melt, stirring until smooth. Drizzle preserves evenly over custard; top each serving with 1 tablespoon whipped topping. Garnish with mint leaves, if desired. Yield: 8 servings.

Points: 5; **Exchanges:** 2 Starch, 1 Fat
Per serving: CAL 202 (26% from fat); PRO 3.9g; FAT 5.9g (sat 2.1g); CARB 31.7g; FIB 0g; CHOL 54mg; IRON 0.2mg; SOD 101mg; CALC 107mg

---

FAVORITE FAMILY FEAST

Serves 8

Ground Beef-and-Noodle Bake

Mixed Green Salad With
Dijon Dressing

Hot Fudge Sundaes

Ground Beef-and-Noodle Bake

6 ounces uncooked medium egg noodles
1 pound ground round
1 cup sliced mushrooms
⅓ cup chopped onion
2 garlic cloves, minced
2 (8-ounce) cans no-salt-added tomato sauce
½ teaspoon freshly ground pepper
¼ teaspoon salt
1 (12-ounce) carton 1% low-fat cottage cheese
1 (8-ounce) carton fat-free sour cream
⅓ cup chopped green onions
2 tablespoons grated Parmesan cheese
1 tablespoon poppy seeds
¾ cup (3 ounces) shredded reduced-fat sharp cheddar cheese, divided
Cooking spray

1. Cook noodles according to package directions, omitting salt and fat. Drain and set aside.

2. Cook ground round and next 3 ingredients in a large nonstick skillet over medium heat until browned, stirring to crumble. Drain in a colander. Wipe drippings from skillet with a paper towel. Return meat mixture to skillet. Add tomato sauce, pepper, and salt.

3. Combine cottage cheese and next 4 ingredients in a large bowl. Stir in meat mixture, noodles, and ⅓ cup cheddar cheese.

4. Spoon noodle mixture into a 2-quart casserole coated with cooking spray. Cover and chill casserole 8 hours.

5. Preheat oven to 350°.

6. Remove casserole from refrigerator; let stand at room temperature 30 minutes. Bake, covered, at 350° for 20 minutes. Uncover; sprinkle with

remaining cheddar cheese. Bake, uncovered, an additional 5 minutes. Yield: 8 servings.

Points: 6; **Exchanges:** 3 Lean Meat, 1½ Starch
Per serving: CAL 288 (24% from fat); PRO 27.2g; FAT 7.8g (sat 3.2g); CARB 25.8g; FIB 2g; CHOL 65mg; IRON 3mg; SOD 400mg; CALC 174mg

Mixed Green Salad With Dijon Dressing

For a salad that goes together in seconds, prepare the dressing and vegetables ahead of time and buy preshredded cheese.

4   cups torn red leaf lettuce
4   cups torn Bibb lettuce
½   cup (2 ounces) finely shredded fat-free
     mozzarella cheese
2   large tomatoes, cut into wedges
1   large green bell pepper, cut into rings
6   green onions, cut into 1-inch pieces
Dijon Dressing

1. Combine first 6 ingredients in a bowl. Drizzle Dijon Dressing over salad; toss gently to coat. Yield: 8 servings (serving size: 1 cup).

DIJON DRESSING:
¼   cup fat-free mayonnaise
2   tablespoons water
1   tablespoon Dijon mustard
1   tablespoon honey
1   tablespoon cider vinegar
1½ teaspoons vegetable oil
⅛   teaspoon ground red pepper
1   garlic clove, crushed

1. Combine all ingredients in a bowl; stir with a whisk until blended. Cover and chill. Yield: about ⅔ cup.

Points: 1; **Exchanges:** 2 Veg
Per serving: CAL 60 (21% from fat); PRO 3.5g; FAT 1.4g (sat 0.2g); CARB 9.7g; FIB 1.7g; CHOL 1mg; IRON 0.9mg; SOD 211mg; CALC 67mg

Have Ground Beef-and-Noodle Bake ready to pull out when you're short on time. Complete the meal with Mixed Green Salad With Dijon Dressing.

Hot Fudge Sundaes

For just 10 calories more, you can top off your sundae with a cherry.

½ cup sugar
¼ cup unsweetened cocoa
1 tablespoon cornstarch
2 teaspoons instant coffee granules
⅔ cup evaporated skim milk
2 teaspoons margarine
½ teaspoon vanilla extract
4 cups low-fat vanilla ice cream
2 small bananas, sliced
2 teaspoons coarsely chopped pecans

1. Combine sugar, unsweetened cocoa, cornstarch, and instant coffee granules in a medium saucepan. Gradually stir in evaporated skim milk. Bring to a boil over medium heat, and cook 1 minute or until thick, stirring constantly. Remove from heat. Add margarine and vanilla extract, stirring until margarine melts. (**Make-Ahead Tip:** Pour hot fudge sauce into a small bowl, and cover surface of sauce with plastic wrap. Chill up to 24 hours. To reheat, uncover and microwave at HIGH 30 seconds or until warm [do not boil]).

2. Spoon ½ cup vanilla ice cream into each of 8 dessert dishes; top with hot fudge sauce, banana slices, and chopped pecans. Yield: 8 servings.

Points: 4; **Exchanges:** 2 Starch, 1 Fat
Per serving: CAL 193 (20% from fat); PRO 5g; FAT 4.3g (sat 2g); CARB 34.8g; FIB 0.4g; CHOL 10mg; IRON 0.7mg; SOD 90mg; CALC 156mg

---

T V   D I N N E R

Serves 6

Black Bean-and-Smoked Turkey Soup

Marinated Cucumber, Mushroom, and Onion Salad

Herb-Cheese Bread

Vanilla low-fat frozen yogurt and gingersnaps

(½ cup yogurt and 3 gingersnaps per person)

Black Bean-and-Smoked Turkey Soup

Crush cumin seeds with a mortar and pestle, or place seeds in a heavy-duty zip-top plastic bag and crush with a mallet or rolling pin.

1 tablespoon vegetable oil
1 cup chopped red onion
1 cup chopped celery
1 cup chopped carrot
1 tablespoon cumin seeds, crushed
1 teaspoon dried oregano
3 garlic cloves, minced
2 cups water
¾ teaspoon salt
3 (10½-ounce) cans low-salt chicken broth
2 (15-ounce) cans no-salt-added black beans, drained
½ pound smoked fat-free turkey breast, chopped
½ cup chopped red bell pepper
¼ cup chopped fresh or 1 tablespoon dried parsley
2 tablespoons dry sherry
½ teaspoon hot sauce
6 tablespoons low-fat sour cream
Cilantro sprigs (optional)

1. Heat oil in a Dutch oven over medium heat. Add onion and next 5 ingredients; sauté 5 minutes. Stir in water, salt, broth, and beans; bring to a boil. Cover, reduce heat, and simmer 45 minutes or until tender.

2. Place half of bean mixture in a blender or food processor; process until smooth. Return puréed bean mixture to pan. Stir in turkey, bell pepper, parsley, sherry, and hot sauce; cook an additional 5 minutes or until thoroughly heated. (**Make-Ahead Tip:** Prepare soup. Let soup cool, and freeze in an airtight container up to three months, or store in the refrigerator for up to four days in a nonaluminum container. Thaw and reheat over low heat.) Ladle soup into bowls, and top with sour cream. Garnish with cilantro sprigs, if desired. Yield: 6 servings (serving size: 1½ cups soup and 1 tablespoon sour cream).

Points: 4; **Exchanges:** 1 Fat, 1½ Very Lean Meat, 1½ Starch, 1 Veg
Per serving: CAL 223 (24% from fat); PRO 14.9g; FAT 5.9g (sat 2g); CARB 29.5g; FIB 5.3g; CHOL 14mg; IRON 3.8mg; SOD 737 mg; CALC 77mg

Marinated Cucumber, Mushroom, and Onion Salad

To prepare the cucumbers, peel them and cut in half lengthwise. Scoop seeds out of each half with a spoon, and cut into slices.

⅓ cup sherry vinegar
2 teaspoons olive oil
2 teaspoons Dijon mustard
½ teaspoon salt
¼ teaspoon dried oregano
⅛ teaspoon pepper
6 cups peeled seeded sliced cucumber
3 cups sliced mushrooms
1 cup slivered red onion

1. Combine first 6 ingredients in a large bowl; stir well. Add cucumber, mushrooms, and red onion; toss gently. Cover and chill 2 hours. Serve salad with a slotted spoon. Yield: 8 servings (serving size: 1 cup).

Points: 1; **Exchanges:** 2 Veg
Per serving: CAL 49 (26% from fat); PRO 1.4g; FAT 1.4g (sat 0.2g); CARB 6.4g; FIB 1.1g; CHOL 0mg; IRON 0.7mg; SOD 250mg; CALC 23mg

Herb-Cheese Bread

¼ cup reduced-calorie stick margarine
¼ cup minced green onions
2 garlic cloves, crushed
¼ teaspoon dried oregano
¼ teaspoon ground cumin
⅛ teaspoon crushed red pepper
⅛ teaspoon salt
1 (1-pound) loaf Italian bread, cut in half lengthwise
½ cup (2 ounces) shredded reduced-fat Monterey Jack cheese

1. Preheat oven to 400°.

2. Melt margarine in a small skillet over medium-high heat. Add green onions and garlic cloves, and sauté 2 minutes. Remove from heat; stir in dried oregano, ground cumin, crushed red pepper, and salt. Brush margarine mixture evenly over cut sides of Italian bread. Sprinkle cheese over bottom half of loaf, and top with top half of loaf. Wrap in foil. (**Make-Ahead Tip:** Assemble loaf, wrap in foil, and store in refrigerator. Bring to room temperature before

baking.) Bake at 400° for 20 minutes. Serve warm. Yield: 12 servings.

Points: 3; **Exchanges:** 1½ Starch, ½ Fat
Per serving: CAL 140 (23% from fat); PRO 4.9g; FAT 3.6g (sat 1g); CARB 21.8g; FIB 1.1g; CHOL 3mg; IRON 0.9mg; SOD 313mg; CALC 48mg

---

GIRLFRIENDS' LUNCHEON

Serves 6

Tropical Chicken Salad
Miniature Mango Muffins
Chocolate Malted Coffee

Tropical Chicken Salad

1 (8-ounce) can crushed pineapple in juice, drained
¼ cup 1% low-fat cottage cheese
2 tablespoons light mayonnaise
1 teaspoon sugar
2 teaspoons lemon juice
½ teaspoon grated orange rind
¼ teaspoon grated lime rind
⅛ teaspoon ground ginger
3 cups chopped cooked chicken breast
½ cup seedless green grapes
½ cup sliced water chestnuts
1 tablespoon chopped fresh chives
½ cup drained canned mandarin oranges packed in water
6 cups thinly sliced spinach
1 tablespoon slivered almonds, toasted
Fresh chives (optional)
Orange rind curls (optional)

1. Place first 8 ingredients in a food processor, and process until smooth. Combine pineapple mixture, chicken, grapes, water chestnuts, and chopped chives in a bowl; stir well. Gently fold in oranges. Cover and chill up to 8 hours.

2. Divide spinach evenly among 6 salad plates; top evenly with chicken mixture. Sprinkle evenly with almonds. Garnish salad with fresh chives and orange rind curls, if desired. Yield: 6 servings.

Points: 3; **Exchanges:** 3 Very Lean Meat, 1 Veg, ½ Fruit, ½ Fat
Per serving: CAL 171 (24% from fat); PRO 21.3g; FAT 4.5g (sat 0.8g); CARB 11.2g; FIB 1.8g; CHOL 53mg; IRON 1.7mg; SOD 146mg; CALC 54mg

Tropical Chicken Salad,
Miniature Mango Muffins, and
Chocolate Malted Coffee

Miniature Mango Muffins

Mash mango cubes with a fork or potato masher.

½ cup whole-wheat flour
½ cup all-purpose flour
2 tablespoons toasted wheat germ
2 tablespoons firmly packed brown sugar
½ teaspoon baking soda
⅛ teaspoon salt
½ cup mashed mango
1½ tablespoons vegetable oil
2¼ teaspoons skim milk
½ teaspoon rum extract or vanilla extract
¼ teaspoon coconut extract
¼ teaspoon almond extract
1 large egg, lightly beaten
Cooking spray

1. Preheat oven to 350°.

2. Combine first 6 ingredients in a large bowl; make a well in center of mixture. Combine next 7 ingredients; add to dry ingredients, stirring just until moist.

3. Divide batter evenly among miniature (1¾-inch) muffin cups coated with cooking spray. Bake at 350° for 10 minutes or until golden. Remove from pans; let cool on a wire rack. (**Make-Ahead Tip:** Store muffins at room temperature in an airtight container up to 1 day.) Yield: 18 muffins (serving size: 3 muffins).

Points: 3; **Exchanges:** 1½ Starch, 1 Fat
Per serving: CAL 150 (31% from fat); PRO 3.9g; FAT 5.1g (sat 1g); CARB 23.4g; FIB 2.1; CHOL 33mg; IRON 1.2mg; SOD 132mg; CALC 33mg

Chocolate Malted Coffee

Specialty coffees, such as chocolate almond-flavored, are available at specialty coffee shops or are displayed with other coffees in most supermarkets.

4 cups brewed chocolate almond-flavored coffee
1¾ cups skim milk
¼ cup malted milk powder
2 tablespoons chocolate-flavored syrup

1. Combine brewed coffee, skim milk, malted milk powder, and chocolate-flavored syrup in a blender, and process until frothy. Serve drink warm or cold. (**Make-Ahead Tip:** Prepare coffee up to 24 hours in advance. Cover and chill. Serve chilled or reheat in microwave.) Yield: 6 cups (serving size: 1 cup).

Points: 2; **Exchanges:** 1½ Starch
Per serving: CAL 102 (12% from fat); PRO 4.6g; FAT 1.4g (sat 0.8g); CARB 17.9g; FIB 0g; CHOL 1mg; IRON 0.9mg; SOD 108mg; CALC 129mg

S O U P - I T - U P   S U P P E R

Serves 10

Chicken-Corn Soup

Frozen Fruit Salad

Green Onion Drop Biscuits

NO MORE MESSY MANGOES

Peeling and cutting up a mango can create an awful mess. To eliminate most of this mess, use the "pop up" method.

1. Make a lengthwise slice as close to the pit as possible on one side; repeat on other side. You now have two thick mango slices and the pit, surrounded by a small amount of mango flesh.

2. Place one of the thick slices skin side down. For cubes, make vertical and horizontal slashes through the flesh in a tic-tac-toe pattern. For slices, just make horizontal slashes. Cut all the way through the flesh but not through the skin.

3. Hold the sides of the mango slice, flesh side up, and "pop up" the fruit by turning the skin inside out. Cut the flesh away from the skin. Repeat with the second slice. Then peel the skin that remains around the pit, and cut away the flesh attached to the pit. A medium mango yields about 1 cup of cubed or sliced flesh.

Chicken-Corn Soup

12 cups water
1 cup sliced onion
1 cup coarsely chopped celery
1 pound chicken breast halves
½ pound chicken thighs
½ pound chicken drumsticks
3 cups fresh corn kernels or frozen whole-kernel corn, thawed
4 ounces uncooked medium-size egg noodles
¾ teaspoon salt
½ teaspoon pepper
¼ teaspoon saffron threads
1 large egg, lightly beaten
2 tablespoons chopped fresh parsley

1. Combine first 6 ingredients in a large Dutch oven; bring to a boil. Reduce heat, and simmer, uncovered, 1 hour or until chicken is tender. Remove from heat.
2. Remove chicken pieces from broth, and let cool. Remove skin from chicken, and remove chicken from bones; discard skin and bones. Shred meat into bite-size pieces; cover and chill. Strain broth through a sieve into a large bowl, reserving 8 cups; discard solids. Cover and chill broth 8 hours. Skim solidified fat from surface of broth, and discard.
3. Combine broth and chicken in Dutch oven, and bring to a boil. Stir in corn, noodles, salt, pepper, and saffron threads; bring to a boil. Reduce heat, and simmer, uncovered, 10 minutes or until noodles are done. Remove soup from heat. Slowly pour beaten egg into soup, stirring constantly (the egg will form lacy strands as it cooks). Ladle into soup bowls; sprinkle with parsley. Yield: 10 servings (serving size: 1 cup).

Points: 3; **Exchanges:** 1 Starch, 1½ Lean Meat
Per serving: CAL 171 (22% from fat); PRO 14.5g; FAT 4.2 (sat 1.1g); CARB 19.9g; FIB 2g; CHOL 66mg; IRON 1.4mg; SOD 228mg; CALC 22mg

Frozen Fruit Salad

1½ cups seedless red grapes, halved
1½ cups sliced ripe banana (about 3 medium)
1½ cups grapefruit sections (about 2 large)
1½ cups cubed fresh pineapple
1½ cups pineapple juice
⅓ cup frozen orange juice concentrate, thawed and undiluted
¼ cup water

1. Combine all ingredients in a large bowl, and stir well. Pour into a 13- x 9-inch baking dish. Cover and freeze 8 hours or until firm. Let stand at room temperature 1 hour before serving or until slightly thawed. Cut into squares. Yield: 10 servings.

Points: 2; **Exchanges:** 1½ Fruit
Per serving: CAL 100 (4% from fat); PRO 1.2g; FAT 0.4g (sat 0.1g); CARB 25.1g; FIB 1.7g; CHOL 0mg; IRON 0.4mg; SOD 2mg; CALC 23mg

Green Onion Drop Biscuits

A food processor works great to combine dry ingredients and shortening—pulse a few times until the mixture is the size of peas. If you don't have buttermilk, you can substitute plain low-fat yogurt.

2 cups all-purpose flour
2 teaspoons baking powder
½ teaspoon salt
¼ teaspoon baking soda
3 tablespoons vegetable shortening
¼ cup finely chopped green onions
1 cup low-fat buttermilk
Cooking spray

1. Preheat oven to 400°.
2. Combine all-purpose flour, baking powder, salt, and baking soda in a large bowl; cut in shortening with a pastry blender or 2 knives until mixture resembles coarse meal. Stir in green onions. Add low-fat buttermilk, stirring just until moist.
3. Drop batter by heaping tablespoons onto a baking sheet coated with cooking spray. Bake at 400° for 15 minutes or until lightly browned. (**Make-Ahead Tip:** Store biscuits at room temperature in an airtight container up to 1 day.) Yield: 16 biscuits (serving size: 1 biscuit).

Points: 2; **Exchanges:** 1 Starch, ½ Fat
Per serving: CAL 111 (26% from fat); PRO 2.9g; FAT 3.2g (sat 1g); CARB 17.2g; FIB 0.6g; CHOL 0mg; IRON 1.1mg; SOD 135mg; CALC 74mg

*C*utting corn off the cob can be time-consuming, but the flavor of fresh corn is worth every minute.

1 Whole-kernel
Hold corn with stem resting on bottom of bowl. Beginning at the top, cut along the cob through the kernels.

2 Cream-style
Cut away only the tops of the kernels. Use the dull side of a knife to scrape the cob, removing all of the "milk."

3 Grated
Place a metal grater with large holes in a bowl, and rub the ear firmly down the side of the grater.

Mexican Turkey Sandwiches

Individually wrapped Mexican Turkey Sandwiches are perfectly portable.

⅔ cup light cream cheese, softened
¼ cup chopped onion
¼ cup no-salt-added salsa
2   tablespoons chopped ripe olives
6   (6-inch) flour tortillas
10 ounces thinly sliced smoked turkey breast
6   tablespoons no-salt-added salsa
½ cup (2 ounces) shredded fat-free cheddar cheese
1   cup thinly sliced curly leaf lettuce

1. Beat cream cheese at medium speed of a mixer until smooth. Add next 3 ingredients; stir well.

2. Spread cream cheese mixture evenly over tortillas; top evenly with turkey, salsa, cheese, and lettuce. Roll up tortillas jelly-roll fashion. Wrap sandwiches individually with plastic wrap; chill at least 2 hours. Yield: 6 servings.

Points: 5; **Exchanges:** 2 Very Lean Meat, 1 Fat, 1 Starch
Per serving: CAL 213 (32% from fat); PRO 19g; FAT 7.6g (sat 3.2g); CARB 17.6g; FIB 1.5g; CHOL 43mg; IRON 1.4mg; SOD 738mg; CALC 162mg

Vegetable-Pasta Salad

8   ounces uncooked farfalle (bow tie pasta)
1   cup quartered cherry tomatoes

¾ cup frozen green peas, thawed
2 small yellow bell peppers, cut into strips
3½ tablespoons fat-free Italian dressing
2 tablespoons grated Parmesan cheese

1. Cook pasta according to package directions, omitting salt and fat; drain. Rinse pasta under cold water; drain. Combine pasta, tomatoes, peas, and bell pepper in a bowl; toss gently. Combine Italian dressing and cheese; stir well. Drizzle over salad; toss well. Cover and chill up to 8 hours. Yield: 6 servings (serving size: 1 cup).

Points: 3; **Exchanges:** 2 Starch, 1 Vegetable
Per serving: CAL 182 (7% from fat); PRO 7.1g; FAT 1.5g (sat 0.5g); CARB 35.2g; FIB 2.7g; CHOL 1mg; IRON 2.3mg; SOD 153mg; CALC 38mg

Sparkling Fruit Soda

2 cups unsweetened peach juice blend
2 cups apple juice
2 cups chilled lemon-lime sparkling water

1. Combine peach juice and apple juice in a pitcher. Cover and chill up to 24 hours. Just before serving, stir in sparkling water. Serve over ice. Yield: 6 servings (serving size: 1 cup).

Points: 2; **Exchanges:** 1 Fruit, ½ Starch
Per serving: CAL 83 (1% from fat); PRO 0.5g; FAT 0.1g (sat 0g); CARB 20.3g; FIB 0.2g; CHOL 0mg; IRON 0.3mg; SOD 8mg; CALC 17mg

---

C A N T I N A   S U P P E R

Serves 4

Beef, Bean, and Cornbread Casserole

Orange-and-Avocado Salad

Beef, Bean, and Cornbread Casserole

¾ pound 93% ultra-lean ground beef
1 cup chopped onion
1 garlic clove, minced
Cooking spray
1 tablespoon chili powder
1½ teaspoons ground cumin
1 teaspoon sugar

½ teaspoon dried oregano
2 (8-ounce) cans no-salt-added tomato sauce
1 (16-ounce) can pinto beans, drained
1 (4.5-ounce) can chopped green chiles, drained
¾ cup skim milk
1 large egg, lightly beaten
1⅓ cups self-rising yellow cornmeal mix

1. Preheat oven to 400°.
2. Cook beef, onion, and garlic in a large saucepan coated with cooking spray over medium-high heat until browned, stirring to crumble beef. Drain and return beef mixture to saucepan. Stir in chili powder and next 6 ingredients. Reduce heat to medium low; cover and cook 10 minutes, stirring occasionally. Pour mixture into a 2-quart casserole coated with cooking spray; set aside.
3. Combine milk and egg in a medium bowl; stir well. Add cornmeal mix, and stir well. Pour cornmeal mixture over casserole. Bake at 400° for 20 minutes or until cornbread topping is lightly browned. Yield: 4 servings.

Note: If self-rising yellow cornmeal is not available in your area, you may make your own by combining 1⅓ cups yellow cornmeal, 2 teaspoons baking powder, and ½ teaspoon salt.

Make-Ahead Tip: You can assemble the casserole ahead of time, omitting the cornbread topping. Cover casserole and chill in refrigerator or freeze (thaw frozen casserole overnight in the refrigerator). Let casserole stand at room temperature for 30 minutes. Add cornbread topping, and bake as directed.

Points: 9; **Exchanges:** 2½ Lean Meat, 4 Starch
Per serving: CAL 448 (18% from fat); PRO 29.7g; FAT 9g (sat 2.9g); CARB 64.8g; FIB 4.4g; CHOL 108mg; IRON 6.7mg; SOD 948mg; CALC 274mg

Orange-and-Avocado Salad

4 cups torn curly leaf lettuce
1 cup fresh orange sections (about 3 large)
½ cup peeled chopped avocado

2 tablespoons water
1½ teaspoons sugar
4 teaspoons white wine vinegar
¼ teaspoon salt
¼ teaspoon pepper
¼ teaspoon hot pepper sauce

1. Combine curly leaf lettuce, orange sections, and avocado in a bowl; toss gently. Combine water and next 5 ingredients in a small bowl; stir with a whisk until blended. Pour over salad, and toss gently to coat. Yield: 4 servings (serving size: 2 cups).

Points: 1; **Exchanges:** 2 Veg, ½ Fat
Per serving: CAL 66 (44% from fat); PRO 1.5g; FAT 3.2g (sat 0.5g); CARB 9.2g; FIB 2.6g; CHOL 0mg; IRON 0.4mg; SOD 179mg; CALC 19mg

Begin your dinner under the stars with Spiced Cranberry Sipper.

Spiced Cranberry Sipper

1   cup cranberry juice cocktail
1   cup apple juice
1   cup water
¼   cup sugar
1   tablespoon orange juice
2   whole cloves
1   (3-inch) cinnamon sticks
Orange rind curls (optional)

1. Combine cocktail, apple juice, water, sugar, orange juice, cloves, and cinnamon sticks in a saucepan, stirring until sugar dissolves. Bring to a simmer; cover and cook 20 minutes. Discard cloves and cinnamon sticks. Serve chilled. Garnish with orange rind curls, if desired. Yield: 4 servings (serving size: ¾ cup).

Note: For a Spiced Cranberry Cocktail, add 1 tablespoon vodka to each serving; the calories go up to 150 per serving.

Points: 2; Exchanges: 2 Fruit
Per serving: CAL 117 (1% from fat); PRO 0.1g; FAT 0.1g (sat 0g); CARB 29.8g; FIB 0.1g; CHOL 0mg; IRON 0.3mg; SOD 5mg; CALC 7mg

Mediterranean Lentil Salad

1   cup lentils
4   cups water
3   large red bell peppers (about 1½ pounds)
¼   cup balsamic vinegar
¼   cup low-salt chicken broth
1   tablespoon olive oil
1   teaspoon dried basil
¼   teaspoon salt
¼   teaspoon pepper
1   garlic clove, minced
8   romaine lettuce leaves
¼   cup (1 ounce) crumbled goat cheese

1. Combine lentils and water in a saucepan; bring to a boil. Cover, reduce heat, and simmer 25 minutes or until tender; drain. Rinse under cold running water; drain and set aside.

2. Cut red bell peppers in half lengthwise; discard seeds and membranes. Place bell peppers, skin side up, on a foil-lined baking sheet, and flatten with hand. Broil 10 minutes or until blackened. Place in a zip-top plastic bag, and seal. Let stand 5 minutes. Peel and cut into 2- x ½-inch strips.

3. Combine lentils, bell pepper strips, balsamic vinegar, and next 6 ingredients in a large bowl; toss gently. Cover and chill 2 hours. Spoon onto lettuce-lined plates, and top with cheese. Yield: 4 servings (serving size: 1 cup salad and 1 tablespoon cheese).

Points: 4; Exchanges: 1½ Very Lean Meat, 2 Starch, 1 Fat
Per serving: CAL 246 (22% from fat); PRO 15.8g; FAT 6g (sat 1.7g); CARB 34.2g; FIB 7.5g; CHOL 6mg; IRON 6mg; SOD 243mg; CALC 76mg

Almond Cakes

1   cup blanched almonds
1⅓ cups sugar
1   cup all-purpose flour
1   teaspoon rose water (optional)
3   large egg whites
Cooking spray

1. Preheat oven to 325°.

2. Place almonds in a food processor; process until finely ground. Add sugar and flour; process until blended. Add rose water, if desired, and egg whites; process until well blended (mixture will be very thick). With floured hands, shape the dough into 28 balls, and place 2 inches apart on baking sheets coated with cooking spray. Bake at 325° for 28 minutes or until crisp on the outside and soft on the inside. Remove from pans; let cool on wire racks. Yield: 28 cookies (serving size: 1 cookie).

Points: 2; Exchanges: 1 Starch, ½ Fat
Per serving: CAL 88 (32% from fat); PRO 2.2g; FAT 3.1g (sat 0.3g); CARB 13.5g; FIB 0.9g; CHOL 0mg; IRON 0.5mg; SOD 6mg; CALC 15mg

Make the Most of It

THESE ORIGINAL MENUS DELIVER MAXIMUM
EATING SATISFACTION USING MINIMAL POINTS.

*I*f *you're using the 1•2•3 Success Plan to lose weight, you're probably enjoying the plan's flexibility. Because no foods are off-limits, you can eat whatever you want as long as you stay within your personal Points range. But you're probably searching for ways to get the most out of your range as well as strategies for incorporating the occasional splurge.*

Problem solved. All of the menus—not recipes—in this chapter are 8 Points or fewer. Maybe you and some co-workers celebrated a job well done with an extravagant lunch that used most of your day's Points. No problem. Try the Honey-Dijon Grilled Pork Tenderloin menu (8 Points) for dinner. Got a dinner date tonight? Pack the Chicken Fiesta Salad menu (7 Points) for lunch and your date can buy you dessert too. We've even included a menu for a low-Point breakfast—Three-Bran Muffins, apple wedges, and a Banana Split Smoothie (6 Points total)—to jump-start your day. And because each food's Point value is based on the amount of calories, fat, and fiber it contains, these recipes will help you eat more nutritiously. Now getting with the program—and sticking with it—is easier than ever.

**One serving of
Hearty Three-Bean
Chili provides more
than 8 grams of fiber.**

CLASSMATES' REUNION

Serves 8

Hearty Three-Bean Chili

Marinated Vegetable Salad

Colorful Corn Muffins

Menu Points Per Serving: 7

Hearty Three-Bean Chili

1   teaspoon vegetable oil
2   cups chopped onion
3   garlic cloves, minced
2   tablespoons chili powder
1½ tablespoons ground cumin
½   teaspoon salt
2   (14½-ounce) cans no-salt-added stewed
    tomatoes, undrained
2   (15-ounce) cans black beans, drained
1   (16-ounce) can kidney beans, drained
1   (15-ounce) can pinto beans, drained
1   (14¼-ounce) can fat-free beef broth
½   cup water
1   large green bell pepper, cut into 1-inch
    pieces
1   large red bell pepper, cut into 1-inch pieces
½   cup fat-free sour cream
⅓   cup diced green bell pepper
⅓   cup diced red bell pepper

1. Heat oil in a large Dutch oven over medium-high heat. Add onion and garlic; sauté 5 minutes or until tender. Stir in chili powder, cumin, and salt; sauté 1 minute. Add tomatoes and next 7 ingredients; bring to a boil. Cover, reduce heat, and simmer 30 minutes, stirring occasionally. Spoon chili into bowls; top each serving with 1 tablespoon sour cream. Sprinkle diced green and red bell pepper evenly over each serving. Yield: 8 servings (serving size: 1½ cups).

Points: 4; **Exchanges:** ½ Very Lean Meat, 2½ Starch, 2 Veg
Per serving: CAL 276 (13% from fat); PRO 14.7g; FAT 3.9g (sat 1.5g); CARB 48.3g; FIB 8.1g; CHOL 6mg; IRON 5.7mg; SOD 535mg; CAL 120mg

Marinated Vegetable Salad

2⅔ cups small cauliflower florets
1½ cups diagonally sliced carrot
1⅓ cups diagonally sliced celery
⅔   cup sliced red bell pepper
⅓   cup sliced ripe olives
1   (14-ounce) can quartered artichoke hearts,
    drained
½   cup white wine vinegar
1   tablespoon olive oil
1¼ teaspoons dried Italian seasoning
¼   teaspoon crushed red pepper

1. Steam cauliflower and carrot, covered, 3 minutes or until crisp-tender. Rinse under cold water, and drain. Combine cauliflower mixture, celery, and next 3 ingredients in a bowl; toss gently. Combine vinegar and next 3 ingredients in a bowl; stir well. Pour over vegetables, and toss gently to coat. Cover and chill. Yield: 8 servings (serving size: 1 cup).

Points: 1; **Exchanges:** 2 Veg, ½ Fat
Per serving: CAL 69 (34% from fat); PRO 2.8g; FAT 2.6g (sat 0.4g); CARB 11.4g; FIB 2.6g; CHOL 0mg; IRON 1.6mg; SOD 202mg; CALC 56mg

Colorful Corn Muffins

1¼ cups all-purpose flour
¾   cup yellow cornmeal
1   tablespoon sugar
2   teaspoons baking powder
¼   teaspoon salt
¼   teaspoon ground red pepper
1   cup low-fat buttermilk
2   tablespoons margarine, melted
1   large egg, lightly beaten
½   cup diced red bell pepper
⅓   cup thinly sliced green onions
1   tablespoon minced seeded jalapeño pepper
Cooking spray

1. Preheat oven to 400°.
2. Combine first 6 ingredients in a medium bowl; make a well in center of mixture. Combine buttermilk, margarine, and egg; add to dry ingredients, stirring just until moist. Fold in bell pepper, green onions, and jalapeño pepper.
3. Divide batter evenly among muffin cups coated with cooking spray. Bake at 400° for 28 minutes or until golden. Remove from pans immediately. Yield: 12 muffins (serving size: 1 muffin).

Note: Store remaining corn muffins in an airtight container at room temperature up to 2 days, or freeze up to 1 month.

Points: 2; **Exchanges:** 1 Starch, ½ Fat
Per serving: CAL 119 (22% from fat); PRO 3.5g; FAT 2.9g (sat 0.6g); CARB 19.6g; FIB 1g; CHOL 19mg; IRON 1.2mg; SOD 99mg; CALC 77mg

SUPPER WITH THE KIDS

Serves 4

Inside-Out Pizza

Apple wedges
(4 wedges per person)

Orange-Butterscotch Cookies

Menu Points Per Serving: 8

Inside-Out Pizza

A pizza sandwich? Kids will love it! You can slice some apples or toss a salad for a quick side dish.

1   cup bread flour
½   cup whole-wheat flour
½   teaspoon sugar
¼   teaspoon salt
1   package dry yeast
⅔   cup hot water (120° to 130°)
½   teaspoon olive oil
1   tablespoon bread flour
Cooking spray
¼   pound ground round
1   cup chopped onion
1   garlic clove, minced
1   cup fat-free spaghetti sauce
⅛   teaspoon salt
½   cup (2 ounces) shredded part-skim mozzarella cheese

1. Combine first 5 ingredients in a large bowl; stir well. Gradually add hot water and oil, beating at low speed of a mixer until blended. Beat at medium speed an additional 2 minutes.

2. Sprinkle 1 tablespoon bread flour evenly over work surface. Turn dough out onto floured surface; knead until smooth and elastic (approximately 5 minutes). Place dough in a large bowl coated with cooking spray, turning to coat top. Cover and let dough rise in a warm place (85°),

Bell pepper and jalapeño add color and flavor to Colorful Corn Muffins.

free from drafts, 1 hour or until doubled in bulk.

3. Punch dough down; turn out onto work surface, and knead lightly 4 or 5 times. Press dough onto a 12-inch pizza pan coated with cooking spray; set aside.

4. Preheat oven to 375°.

5. Coat a large nonstick skillet with cooking spray; place over medium-high heat until hot. Add ground beef, onion, and garlic; cook until beef is browned, stirring to crumble. Drain and return to skillet. Add spaghetti sauce and salt; bring to a boil. Cover, reduce heat, and simmer 10 minutes, stirring occasionally.

6. Spoon meat mixture over half of dough in pizza pan, leaving a ½-inch border. Sprinkle cheese over meat mixture, and moisten edge of dough with water. Fold other half of dough over meat mixture to form a half circle; seal edges of dough by firmly pressing with a fork dipped in flour. Bake at 375° for 20 minutes or until golden. Cut pizza into 4 wedges. Serve warm. Yield: 4 servings.

Points: 6; Exchanges: 1 Lean Meat, 3 Starch, 1 Veg
Per serving: CAL 306 (17% from fat); PRO 16.8g; FAT 5.8g (sat 2.4g); CARB 47.6g; FIB 5.3g; CHOL 26mg; IRON 3.2mg; SOD 523mg; CALC 117mg

Grouper With Fruit-and-Pepper Salsa combines the flavors of the Caribbean.

Orange-Butterscotch Cookies

6   tablespoons stick margarine, softened
½   cup sugar
½   cup firmly packed brown sugar
¼   cup egg substitute
2   tablespoons skim milk
1   teaspoon grated orange rind
1   tablespoon orange juice
1½   cups all-purpose flour
2   teaspoons baking powder
½   teaspoon salt
¼   teaspoon ground nutmeg
⅓   cup butterscotch chips
Cooking spray

1. Preheat oven to 375°.

2. Beat margarine at medium speed of a mixer until creamy; gradually add sugars, beating well. Add egg substitute and next 3 ingredients; beat well.

3. Combine flour and next 3 ingredients. Add to margarine mixture, stirring just until blended. Stir in butterscotch chips. Drop dough by level tablespoons, 2 inches apart, onto baking sheets coated with cooking spray. Bake at 375° for 7 minutes or until edges are golden. Let cool on pans 1 minute. Remove cookies from pans; let cool completely on wire racks. Yield: 40 cookies (serving size: 1 cookie).

Note: Store remaining cookies in an airtight container at room temperature up to 1 week.

Points: 1; Exchanges: ½ Starch, ½ Fat
Per serving: CAL 63 (31% from fat); PRO 0.7g; FAT 2.2g (sat 0.6g); CARB 10g; FIB 0.1g; CHOL 0mg; IRON 0.4mg; SOD 54mg; CALC 21mg

TROPICAL SEAFOOD SUPPER

Serves 6

Grouper With Fruit-and-Pepper Salsa

Saffron Rice

Mixed green salad
(1 cup mixed salad greens and 1 tablespoon fat-free dressing per person)

Pear-Lemon Sorbet

Menu Points Per Serving: 6

Grouper With Fruit-and-Pepper Salsa

½ cup chopped fresh pineapple
⅓ cup chopped green bell pepper
⅓ cup chopped red bell pepper
⅓ cup chopped yellow bell pepper
1 kiwifruit, peeled and thinly sliced
1 tablespoon white wine vinegar
1½ teaspoons water
1 teaspoon brown sugar
1 teaspoon peeled grated fresh ginger
⅛ teaspoon crushed red pepper
2 tablespoons lemon juice
¼ teaspoon curry powder
⅛ teaspoon salt
3 (8-ounce) grouper fillets, halved
Cooking spray

1. Combine first 10 ingredients in a bowl; stir well. Cover and chill at least 2 hours.

2. Combine lemon juice, curry powder, and salt; brush evenly over fillets. Place fillets on a broiler pan coated with cooking spray; broil 8 minutes or until fish flakes easily when tested with a fork. Spoon salsa evenly over fillets. Yield: 6 servings.

Points: 3; **Exchanges:** 3 Very Lean Meat, ½ Starch
Per serving: CAL 140 (10% from fat); PRO 24.6g; FAT 1.6g (sat 0.3g); CARB 5.8g; FIB 1.1g; CHOL 46mg; IRON 1.6mg; SOD 102mg; CALC 28mg

Saffron Rice

Cooking spray
⅓ cup chopped onion
2 garlic cloves, minced
1 cup uncooked long-grain rice
2 cups canned fat-free chicken broth
½ teaspoon salt
¼ teaspoon ground saffron

1. Coat a medium saucepan with cooking spray; place over medium-high heat until hot. Add onion and garlic; sauté until tender. Add rice; cook 1 minute, stirring constantly. Stir in broth, salt, and saffron. Bring to a boil. Cover; reduce heat. Simmer 20 minutes or until rice is tender and liquid is absorbed. Yield: 6 servings (serving size: ½ cup).

Points: 2; **Exchanges:** 1½ Starch
Per serving: CAL 126 (3% from fat); PRO 2.5g; FAT 0.3g (sat 0.1g); CARB 26.5g; FIB 0.5g; CHOL 0mg; IRON 1.4mg; SOD 199mg; CALC 12mg

Pear-Lemon Sorbet

2 (16-ounce) cans pear halves in light syrup, undrained
⅓ cup fresh lemon juice
1 teaspoon grated lemon rind
Thin slices of canned or fresh pear (optional)

1. Place first 3 ingredients in a food processor; process until smooth. Pour into a 13- x 9-inch baking dish; freeze until almost firm. Break mixture into chunks. Place frozen chunks in food processor; process until fluffy but not thawed.

2. Spoon sorbet into dessert dishes; garnish with pear slices, if desired. Serve immediately. Yield: 6 servings (serving size: ⅔ cup).

Points: 1; **Exchanges:** 1 Fruit
Per serving: CAL 89 (0% from fat); PRO 0.4g; FAT 0g (sat 0g); CARB 25.1g; FIB 3.7g; CHOL 0mg; IRON 0.3mg; SOD 8mg; CALC 9.3mg

---

SOUTH-OF-THE-BORDER SPREAD

Serves 4

Chicken Fiesta Salad

Mexican Corn Sticks

Strawberries a l'Orange

Menu Points Per Serving: 7

Chicken Fiesta Salad

3 (4-ounce) skinned, boned chicken breast halves
⅓ cup fresh lime juice, divided
Cooking spray
1 teaspoon olive oil
3 tablespoons chopped green onions
1 cup chopped seeded yellow tomato
1 cup chopped red bell pepper
2 tablespoons chopped seeded jalapeño pepper
2 tablespoons water
2 teaspoons honey
2 cups thinly sliced red leaf lettuce
1 cup thinly sliced iceberg lettuce
1 cup thinly sliced Boston lettuce
1 (15-ounce) can black beans, drained
¼ cup fat-free sour cream

1. Combine chicken and 2 tablespoons lime juice in a heavy-duty, zip-top plastic bag; seal bag, and shake to coat chicken. Marinate in refrigerator 2 hours, turning bag occasionally.

2. Coat a large nonstick skillet with cooking spray; add oil, and place over medium-high heat until hot. Add green onions; sauté 1 minute. Add tomato and chopped peppers; sauté 2 minutes. Add remaining lime juice, water, and honey; cook over medium heat until thoroughly heated. Remove from heat; set aside, and keep warm.

3. Remove chicken from marinade; discard marinade. Prepare grill or broiler. Place chicken on grill rack or broiler pan coated with cooking spray, and cook 5 minutes on each side or until done. Cut chicken into thin slices; set aside, and keep warm.

4. Combine lettuces in a bowl; toss well. Divide lettuce mixture evenly among salad plates; top with black beans. Arrange chicken evenly over beans. Spoon tomato mixture over chicken, and top each serving with 1 tablespoon sour cream. Yield: 4 servings.

Points: 4; **Exchanges:** 2 Veg, 2 Very Lean Meat, 1 Starch, ½ Fat
Per serving: CAL 249 (17% from fat); PRO 27.5g; FAT 4.6g (sat 0.9g); CARB 25.2g; FIB 4.5g; CHOL 54mg; IRON 3.2mg; SOD 223mg; CALC 58mg

Mexican Corn Sticks

¾ cup yellow cornmeal
¾ cup all-purpose flour
1 teaspoon ground cumin
¾ teaspoon baking powder
½ teaspoon baking soda
½ teaspoon chili powder
¼ teaspoon salt
1 (8¾-ounce) can no-salt-added whole-kernel corn, drained
½ cup low-fat buttermilk
¼ cup egg substitute
¼ cup canned chopped green chiles, drained
2 tablespoons margarine, melted
Cooking spray

1. Preheat oven to 425°.
2. Combine first 7 ingredients in a large bowl; make a well in center of mixture. Combine corn, buttermilk, egg substitute, green chiles, and mar-

garine; add corn mixture to dry ingredients, stirring just until moist.

3. Place cast-iron corn stick pans in a 425° oven for 5 minutes or until hot. Coat pans with cooking spray, and immediately spoon batter evenly into hot pans. Bake at 425° for 12 minutes or until corn sticks are golden. Remove from pans immediately. Yield: 15 corn sticks (serving size: 2 corn sticks).

Note: Store remaining corn sticks in an airtight container at room temperature up to 2 days, or freeze up to 1 month.

Points: 3; **Exchanges:** 1½ Starch, 1 Fat
Per serving: CAL 160 (24% from fat); PRO 4.4g; FAT 4.2g (sat 0.2g); CARB 25.6g; FIB 1.4g; CHOL 0mg; IRON 1.6mg; SOD 388mg; CALC 36mg

Strawberries a l'Orange

1 tablespoon grated orange rind
2 tablespoons fresh orange juice
1 tablespoon Cointreau (orange-flavored liqueur) or thawed orange juice concentrate
1 teaspoon sugar
2¼ cups fresh strawberries, halved

1. Combine first 4 ingredients in a medium bowl; stir well. Add strawberries, stirring gently to coat. Cover and chill. Stir well before serving; divide strawberries and syrup evenly among dessert dishes. Yield: 4 servings.

Points: 0; **Exchanges:** ½ Fruit
Per serving: CAL 46 (6% from fat); PRO 0.6g; FAT 0.3g (sat 0g); CARB 9.6g; FIB 2.3g; CHOL 0mg; IRON 0.3; SOD 1mg; CALC 16mg

---

SOUP-AND-SALAD SUPPER

Serves 8

Bean-and-Hominy Soup

Romaine salad
(1 cup sliced romaine lettuce
with 1 tablespoon fat-free
Italian dressing per person)

Mocha Chip Cookies

Menu Points Per Serving: 8

Bean-and-Hominy Soup

3   (15½-ounce) cans Great Northern beans,
    undrained
1   (15½-ounce) can hominy, undrained
1   (14½-ounce) can no-salt-added stewed
    tomatoes, undrained
1   (11½-ounce) can bean with bacon soup,
    undiluted
1   (10-ounce) can diced tomatoes and green
    chiles, undrained
1   (11-ounce) can whole-kernel yellow corn,
    undrained
1⅔ cups water
2   bay leaves
3   tablespoons chopped fresh or 1 tablespoon
    dried cilantro
1   teaspoon ground cumin
1   cup (4 ounces) shredded reduced-fat sharp
    cheddar cheese

1. Combine all ingredients except cheese in a
large Dutch oven, and bring to a boil. Cover,
reduce heat, and simmer 30 minutes, stirring
occasionally. Discard bay leaves. Ladle soup into
bowls, and top with cheddar cheese. Yield: 8
servings (serving size: 1½ cups soup and 1 tablespoon cheese).

Points: 6; **Exchanges:** 4 Starch, 1 Lean Meat
Per serving: CAL 371 (14% from fat); PRO 21g; FAT 5.7g (sat 1.9);
CARB 61.1g; FIB 11.1g; CHOL 10mg; IRON 4.3; SOD 862mg;
CALC 263mg

Mocha Chip Cookies

The flavor of these dark, rich-tasting cookies
gives no hint that they are low in fat.

¼   cup reduced-calorie stick margarine,
    softened
⅓   cup sugar
¼   cup firmly packed brown sugar
¼   cup egg substitute
1   cup all-purpose flour
¼   cup unsweetened cocoa
1   tablespoon instant coffee granules
½   teaspoon baking soda
¼   teaspoon salt

Dinner doesn't get
any easier than Bean-
and-Hominy Soup.

Honey-Dijon Grilled Pork Tenderloin and Snow Peas, Red Pepper, and Pineapple

⅓ cup semisweet chocolate minichips
Cooking spray

1. Preheat oven to 375°.

2. Beat margarine at medium speed of a mixer until creamy; gradually add sugars, beating well. Add egg substitute, and beat well. Combine flour and next 4 ingredients; add flour mixture to margarine mixture, beating just until blended. Stir in chocolate minichips. Drop dough by level tablespoons, 2 inches apart, onto baking sheets coated with cooking spray. Bake at 375° for 5 minutes. Remove from pans, and let cool completely on a wire rack. Yield: 22 cookies (serving size: 1 cookie).

Note: Store remaining cookies in an airtight container at room temperature up to 1 week.

Points: 2; **Exchanges:** ½ Starch, ½ Fat
Per serving: CAL 71 (29% from fat); PRO 1.3g; FAT 2.3g (sat 0.7g); CARB 11.6g; FIB 0.2g; CHOL 0mg; IRON 0.6mg; SOD 81mg; CALC 7mg

---

ORIENTAL WEEKNIGHT SUPPER

Serves 6

Honey-Dijon Grilled Pork Tenderloin

Brown rice
(¹/₂ cup per person)

Snow Peas, Red Pepper, and Pineapple

Menu Points Per Serving: 8

Honey-Dijon Grilled Pork Tenderloin

2 (¾-pound) pork tenderloins
½ cup light beer
3 tablespoons sesame seeds
3 tablespoons honey
2 tablespoons Dijon mustard
½ teaspoon cracked pepper
2 garlic cloves, crushed
Cooking spray
Rosemary sprigs (optional)

1. Trim fat from pork. Combine pork and next 6 ingredients in a large heavy-duty, zip-top plastic bag; seal bag, and shake to coat pork. Marinate pork in refrigerator at least 2 hours, turning bag occasionally.

2. Remove pork from bag, reserving marinade. Insert meat thermometer into thickest portion of 1 tenderloin. Prepare grill or broiler. Place pork on grill rack or broiler pan coated with cooking spray, and cook 25 minutes or until meat thermometer registers 150° (pork will be slightly pink), turning and basting occasionally with reserved marinade. Let pork stand 10 minutes before slicing. Cut each tenderloin diagonally across the grain into thin slices. Garnish with rosemary sprigs, if desired. Yield: 6 servings (serving size: 3 ounces).

Points: 5; **Exchanges:** 3 Lean Meat, ½ Starch
Per serving: CAL 218 (28% from fat); PRO 26.8g; FAT 6.9g (sat 1.8g); CARB 11.3g; FIB 0.3g; CHOL 83mg; IRON 2.1mg; SOD 211mg; CALC 56mg

Snow Peas, Red Pepper, and Pineapple

Cider vinegar blends with pineapple juice and soy sauce to give this colorful side dish a sweet-and-sour twist.

1   (15¼-ounce) can pineapple tidbits in juice, undrained
4   teaspoons cider vinegar
1   tablespoon low-sodium soy sauce
2½ teaspoons cornstarch
2   teaspoons sugar
2¼ cups snow peas (about 10 ounces), trimmed
1   small red bell pepper, cut into ¼-inch-wide strips

1. Drain pineapple tidbits, reserving ½ cup juice. Combine reserved pineapple juice, cider vinegar, soy sauce, cornstarch, and sugar in a large non-stick skillet; stir until mixture is well blended. Place skillet over medium heat, and cook until thick and bubbly, stirring constantly. Stir in pineapple tidbits, snow peas, and red bell pepper strips, and cook 5 minutes or until thoroughly heated. Serve immediately. Yield: 6 servings (serving size: ⅔ cup).

Points: 1; **Exchanges:** 1 Veg, ½ Fruit
Per serving: CAL 68 (4% from fat); PRO 1.3g; FAT 0.3g (sat 0g); CARB 16g; FIB 1.5g; CHOL 0mg; IRON 1.1mg; SOD 84mg; CALC 19mg

---

SUPPER FROM THE GARDEN

Serves 4

Summer Squash Casserole

Steamed new potatoes (3 per person)

Lemon Green Beans

Country Corncakes

Fresh berries
(1 cup assorted fresh berries per person)

Menu Points Per Serving: 8

Summer Squash Casserole

2   pounds yellow squash, sliced
⅔   cup chopped onion
⅓   cup chopped green bell pepper
⅔   cup (2⅔ ounces) shredded reduced-fat cheddar cheese
½   cup egg substitute
1   (4-ounce) jar diced pimiento, drained
¼   teaspoon salt
¼   teaspoon pepper
Cooking spray
3   tablespoons dry breadcrumbs
2   tablespoons chopped fresh parsley
⅛   teaspoon paprika

1. Preheat oven to 350°.

2. Steam squash, onion, and bell pepper, covered, 10 minutes or until vegetables are crisp-tender. Combine steamed vegetables, cheese, and next 4 ingredients in a medium bowl; stir gently. Spoon mixture into a 2-quart casserole coated with cooking spray.

3. Combine breadcrumbs, parsley, and paprika; stir well. Sprinkle over casserole. Bake at 350° for 25 minutes or until thoroughly heated. Yield: 4 servings (serving size: 1 cup).

Points: 2; **Exchanges:** 1 Lean Meat, 2 Veg, ½ Starch
Per serving: CAL 144 (22% from fat); PRO 10.2g; FAT 3.5g (sat 1.2g); CARB 21.8g; FIB 4.8g; CHOL 13mg; IRON 2.8mg; SOD 366mg; CALC 202mg

Lemon Green Beans

½ pound green beans
½ small red bell pepper, cut crosswise into rings
¼ cup water
¼ teaspoon dried basil
1 tablespoon lemon rind strips
1 tablespoon lemon juice
1 teaspoon sesame seeds, toasted

1. Trim ends from beans; remove strings. Cut beans into 2-inch pieces. Combine beans, bell pepper, water, and basil in a saucepan; bring to a boil. Cover, reduce heat, and simmer 12 minutes or until vegetables are tender. Drain well. Spoon into a serving bowl. Add lemon rind, lemon juice, and sesame seeds; toss well. Yield: 4 servings (serving size: ½ cup serving).

Points: 0; **Exchanges:** 1 Veg
Per serving: CAL 25 (18% from fat); PRO 1.3g; FAT 0.5g (sat 0.1g); CARB 5.2g; FIB 1.3g; CHOL 0mg; IRON 0.8mg; SOD 4mg; CALC 33mg

Country Corncakes

1 cup fresh corn kernels (about 2 ears)
1 cup boiling water
½ cup yellow cornmeal
2 teaspoons honey
¼ teaspoon salt
2 large egg whites (at room temperature)

1. Steam corn, covered, 8 minutes or until tender. Drain, and set aside.

2. Combine corn, boiling water, cornmeal, honey, and salt in a medium bowl; stir well. Beat egg whites at high speed of a mixer until stiff peaks form (do not overbeat). Fold egg whites into corn mixture.

3. Spoon about ¼ cup batter for each corncake onto a hot nonstick griddle or nonstick skillet coated with cooking spray. Cook 3 minutes on each side or until brown. Yield: 12 (3½-inch) corncakes (serving size: 3 cakes).

Points: 2; **Exchanges:** 1½ Starch
Per serving: CAL 120 (7% from fat); PRO 4.5g; FAT 0.9g (sat 0g); CARB 24.6g; FIB 1.8g; CHOL 0mg; IRON 0.3mg; SOD 177mg; CALC 1mg

Lemon Green Beans and Country Corncakes showcase summer's bounty.

RUSH-HOUR BREAKFAST

Serves 4

Three-Bran Muffins

Apple wedges
(1 small apple per person)

Banana Split Smoothie

Menu Points Per Serving: 6

Three-Bran Muffins

1 cup shreds of wheat bran cereal (such as All Bran)
½ cup morsels of bran cereal (such as Bran Buds)
½ cup boiling water
¾ cup low-fat buttermilk
½ cup honey
3 tablespoons vegetable oil
1 teaspoon baking soda
4 large egg whites, lightly beaten
1 cup all-purpose flour
1 cup wheat bran
1 teaspoon baking powder
¼ teaspoon salt
¾ cup chopped dates
Cooking spray

1. Preheat oven to 350°.

2. Combine first 3 ingredients in a medium bowl; stir well, and let stand 3 minutes. Add buttermilk and next 4 ingredients; stir well.

3. Combine flour and next 3 ingredients in a large bowl; make a well in center of mixture. Add buttermilk mixture to dry ingredients, stirring just until moist. Fold in dates.

4. Divide batter evenly among muffin cups coated with cooking spray. Bake at 350° for 20 minutes or until a wooden pick inserted in center comes out clean. Yield: 1½ dozen (serving size: 1 muffin).

Note: Store remaining muffins in an airtight container at room temperature up to 2 days, or freeze up to 1 month.

Points: 2; **Exchanges:** 1½ Starch, ½ Fat
Per serving: CAL 123 (21% from fat); PRO 3.3g; FAT 2.9g (sat 0.5g); CARB 25.3g; FIB 4g; CHOL 0mg; IRON 1.4mg; SOD 161mg; CALC 31mg

Banana Split Smoothie

1¼ cups sliced ripe banana (about 2 medium)
1   (8-ounce) can crushed pineapple in juice, undrained
1   cup crushed ice
½   cup orange juice
1   teaspoon sugar
1   (8-ounce) carton vanilla low-fat yogurt

1. Combine first 5 ingredients in a blender; process until smooth. Add yogurt, and process until blended. Serve immediately. Yield: 4 cups (serving size: 1 cup).

Points: 3; **Exchanges:** 1½ Fruit, ½ Sk Milk
Per serving: CAL 138 (7% from fat); PRO 3.7g; FAT 1g (sat 0.5g); CARB 30.7g; FIB 1.7g; CHOL 3mg; IRON 0.4mg; SOD 39mg; CALC 110mg

---

EASY FALL MENU

Serves 4

Tenderloin Steaks With
Pepper Jelly Sauce

Lemon Pepper Veggies

Baked potato (1 small per person)

Menu Points Per Serving: 8

Tenderloin Steaks With Pepper Jelly Sauce

4   (4-ounce) beef tenderloin steaks (1 inch thick)
¾   teaspoon chili powder
½   teaspoon garlic powder
½   teaspoon coarsely ground pepper
¼   teaspoon salt
¼   teaspoon dried oregano
¼   teaspoon ground cumin
1   teaspoon vegetable oil
½   cup no-salt-added beef broth
¼   cup balsamic vinegar
2   tablespoons red jalapeño pepper jelly

1. Trim fat from steaks. Combine chili powder and next 5 ingredients; stir well. Rub chili powder mixture over both sides of steaks.

2. Heat oil in a nonstick skillet over medium-high heat 2 minutes. Add steaks; cook 4 minutes on each side or until desired degree of doneness.

3. Remove steaks from skillet; set aside, and keep warm. Add broth, vinegar, and jelly to skillet; cook 5 minutes or until slightly thick, stirring frequently. Spoon sauce over steaks. Yield: 4 servings (serving size: 1 steak and 1 tablespoon sauce).

Points: 5; **Exchanges:** 3 Lean Meat, ½ Starch
Per serving: CAL 212 (37% from fat); PRO 23.8g; FAT 8.7g (sat 3.2g); CARB 8.2g; FIB 0.3g; CHOL 70mg; IRON 3.5mg; SOD 215mg; CALC 15mg

Lemon Pepper Veggies

2   cups broccoli florets
2   cups cauliflower florets
1   cup thinly sliced carrot
1½ tablespoons reduced-calorie stick margarine, melted
1   tablespoon lemon pepper
½   teaspoon garlic powder

1. Steam first 3 ingredients, covered, 5 minutes; set aside, and keep warm.

2. Combine margarine, lemon pepper, and garlic powder in a large bowl; stir well. Add vegetables; toss gently. Yield: 4 servings (serving size: 1 cup).

Points: 1; **Exchanges:** 2 Veg, ½ Fat
Per serving: CAL 60 (36% from fat); PRO 2.8g; FAT 2.4g (sat 0.4g); CARB 8.9g; FIB 3.9g; CHOL 0mg; IRON 1.3mg; SOD 82mg; CALC 51mg

INGREDIENT	SUBSTITUTION

BAKING PRODUCTS

Baking powder, 1 teaspoon
- ½ teaspoon cream of tartar plus ¼ teaspoon baking soda

Chocolate

  semisweet, 1 ounce
- 1 ounce unsweetened chocolate plus 1 tablespoon sugar

  unsweetened, 1 ounce or square
- 3 tablespoons cocoa plus 1 tablespoon butter or vegetable shortening

  chips, semisweet, 1 ounce
- 1 ounce sweet cooking chocolate

  chips, semisweet, 6-ounce package, melted
- 2 ounces unsweetened chocolate, 2 tablespoons vegetable shortening, and ½ cup sugar

Coconut

  flaked, 1 tablespoon
- 1½ tablespoons grated fresh coconut

  milk, 1 cup
- 1 cup whole or 2% reduced-fat milk

Corn syrup, light-colored, 1 cup
- 1 cup sugar and ¼ cup water
- 1 cup honey

Cornstarch, 1 tablespoon (for thickening)
- 2 tablespoons all-purpose flour
- 2 tablespoons granular tapioca

Cracker crumbs, ¾ cup
- 1 cup dry breadcrumbs

Flour

  all-purpose, 1 tablespoon
- 1½ teaspoons cornstarch, potato starch, or rice starch
- 1½ tablespoons whole-wheat flour
- ½ tablespoon whole-wheat flour and ½ tablespoon all-purpose flour

  all-purpose, 1 cup sifted
  Note: Specialty flours added to
  yeast bread will result in a heavier
  product with reduced volume.
- 1 cup plus 2 tablespoons sifted cake flour
- 1 cup minus 2 tablespoons all-purpose flour (unsifted)
- 1½ cups breadcrumbs
- 1 cup regular oats
- ⅓ cup cornmeal or soybean flour and ⅔ cup all-purpose flour
- ¾ cup whole-wheat flour or bran flour and ¼ cup all-purpose flour

  cake, 1 cup sifted
- 1 cup minus 2 tablespoons all-purpose flour

  self-rising, 1 cup
- 1 cup all-purpose flour, 1 teaspoon baking powder, and ½ teaspoon salt

Marshmallows, miniature, 1 cup
- 10 large

Pecans, chopped, 1 cup
- 1 cup regular oats, toasted (in baked products)

Sugar

  brown, 1 cup firmly packed
- 1 cup granulated sugar

  granulated, 1 teaspoon
- ⅛ teaspoon noncaloric sweetener solution or follow manufacturer's directions

  granulated, 1 cup
- 1 cup corn syrup (decrease liquid called for in recipe by ¼ cup)
- 1⅓ cups molasses (decrease liquid called for in recipe by ⅓ cup)
- 1 cup firmly packed brown sugar
- 1 cup honey (decrease liquid called for in recipe by ¼ cup)

  powdered, 1 cup
- 1 cup granulated sugar and 1 tablespoon cornstarch (processed in food processor)

Vegetable shortening, melted, 1 cup
- 1 cup cooking oil (cooking oil should not be substituted if recipe does not call for melted shortening)

Vegetable shortening, solid, 1 cup (used in baking)
- 1⅛ cups margarine (decrease salt called for in recipe by ½ teaspoon)

Yeast, dry, 1 tablespoon
- 1 cake yeast, compressed
- 1 (¼-ounce) package dry yeast

DAIRY PRODUCTS

Butter, 1 cup
- 1 cup stick margarine

Egg

  1 large
- ¼ cup egg substitute

  2 large
- 3 small eggs

  white, 1 (2 tablespoons)
- 2 tablespoons egg substitute
- 2 teaspoons sifted, dry egg white powder and 2 tablespoons warm water

  yolk, 1 (1½ tablespoons)
- 2 tablespoons sifted, dry egg yolk powder and 2 teaspoons water

Milk

  low-fat buttermilk, 1 cup
- 1 tablespoon vinegar or lemon juice and skim milk to equal 1 cup (allow to stand 5 to 10 minutes)
- 1 cup plain low-fat yogurt
- 1 cup skim milk and 1¾ teaspoons cream of tartar

  skim, 1 cup
- 4 to 5 tablespoons nonfat dry milk powder and enough water to make 1 cup, or follow manufacturer's directions
- ½ cup evaporated skim milk and ½ cup water

  fat-free sweetened, condensed, 1 cup
- Add 1 cup plus 2 tablespoons non-fat dry milk powder to ½ cup warm water. Stir well. Add ¾ cup sugar, and stir until smooth.

INGREDIENT	SUBSTITUTION
Sour cream, fat-free, 1 cup	• 1 cup plain fat-free yogurt and 1 tablespoon cornstarch
	• 1 tablespoon lemon juice and evaporated skim milk to equal 1 cup
Yogurt, plain low-fat, 1 cup	• 1 cup low-fat buttermilk

FRUIT & VEGETABLE PRODUCTS

Lemon	
1 medium	• 2 to 3 tablespoons juice and 1 to 2 teaspoons grated rind
juice, 1 teaspoon	• ½ teaspoon vinegar
Orange, 1 medium	• 6 to 8 tablespoons juice and 2 to 3 tablespoons grated rind
Mushrooms, 1 pound fresh	• 1 (8-ounce) can sliced mushrooms, drained
	• 3 ounces dried mushrooms, rehydrated
Onion, chopped, 1 medium	• 1 tablespoon instant minced onion
	• 1 tablespoon onion powder
Bell pepper	
red or green, chopped, 3 tablespoons	• 1 tablespoon dried red or green bell pepper flakes, rehydrated
red, chopped, 3 tablespoons	• 2 tablespoons diced pimiento
Shallots, chopped, 3 tablespoons	• 2 tablespoons chopped onion and 1 tablespoon chopped garlic
Tomatoes	
fresh, chopped, 2 cups	• 1 (16-ounce) can (may need to drain)
juice, 1 cup	• ½ cup tomato sauce and ½ cup water
Tomato sauce, 2 cups	• ¾ cup tomato paste and 1 cup water

MISCELLANEOUS

Brandy, 1 tablespoon	• ¼ teaspoon brandy extract and 1 tablespoon water
Broth, beef or chicken	
canned broth, 1 cup	• 1 bouillon cube dissolved in 1 cup boiling water
	• 1 cup homemade broth
Chili sauce, 1 cup	• 1 cup tomato sauce, ¼ cup firmly packed brown sugar, 2 tablespoons vinegar, ¼ teaspoon cinnamon, dash of ground cloves, and dash of allspice
Gelatin, flavored, 3-ounce package	• 1 tablespoon unflavored gelatin and 2 cups fruit juice
Honey, 1 cup	• 1¼ cups sugar and ¼ cup water
Ketchup, 1 cup	• 1 cup tomato sauce, ½ cup granulated sugar, and 2 tablespoons white vinegar (for use in cooking)
Macaroni, uncooked, 2 cups (4 cups, cooked)	• 2 cups uncooked spaghetti
	• 4 cups uncooked egg noodles
Mayonnaise, light, 1 cup (for salads and dressings)	• ½ cup plain fat-free yogurt and ½ cup light mayonnaise
	• 1 cup low-fat sour cream
	• 1 cup 1% low-fat cottage cheese pureed in a blender
Rice, uncooked, 1 cup regular (3 cups cooked)	• 1 cup uncooked converted rice
	• 1 cup uncooked brown rice
Vinegar, balsamic, ½ cup	• ½ cup red wine vinegar (slight flavor difference)

SEASONING PRODUCTS

Allspice, ground, 1 teaspoon	• ½ teaspoon ground cinnamon and ½ teaspoon ground cloves
Chives, fresh, chopped, 1 tablespoon	• 1 tablespoon chopped green onion tops
Garlic, 1 clove, small	• ⅛ teaspoon garlic powder or minced dried garlic
Garlic salt, 1 teaspoon	• ⅛ teaspoon garlic powder and ⅞ teaspoon salt
Herbs, fresh, chopped, 1 tablespoon	• 1 teaspoon dried herbs or ¼ teaspoon ground herbs
Horseradish, fresh, grated, 1 tablespoon	• 2 tablespoons prepared horseradish
Mustard, dried, 1 teaspoon	• 1 tablespoon prepared mustard
Onion powder, 1 tablespoon	• 1 medium onion, chopped
	• 1 tablespoon instant minced onion
Parsley, dried, 1 teaspoon	• 1 tablespoon chopped fresh parsley
Pimiento, chopped, 2 tablespoons	• 1 tablespoon dried red pepper flakes, rehydrated
	• 2 to 3 tablespoons chopped red bell pepper
Pumpkin pie spice, 1 teaspoon	• ½ teaspoon ground cinnamon, ¼ teaspoon ground ginger, ⅛ teaspoon ground allspice, and ⅛ teaspoon ground nutmeg
Vanilla bean, 1 (1-inch) piece	• 1 teaspoon vanilla extract
Worcestershire sauce, 1 teaspoon	• 1 teaspoon bottled steak sauce

FOOD	WEIGHT (OR COUNT)	YIELD
Apples	1 pound (3 medium)	3 cups sliced
Bananas	1 pound (3 medium)	2½ cups sliced or about 2 cups mashed
Bread	1 pound	12 to 16 slices
	About 1½ slices	1 cup fresh breadcrumbs
Cabbage	1 pound head	4½ cups shredded
Carrots	1 pound	3 cups shredded
Cheese, American or cheddar	1 pound	About 4 cups shredded
cottage	1 pound	2 cups
cream	3- ounce package	6 tablespoons
Chocolate chips	6- ounce package	1 cup
Cocoa	1 pound	4 cups
Coconut, flaked or shredded	1 pound	5 cups
Coffee	1 pound	80 tablespoons (40 cups perked)
Corn	2 medium ears	1 cup kernels
Cornmeal	1 pound	3 cups
Crab, in shell	1 pound	¾ to 1 cup flaked
Crackers, chocolate wafers	19 wafers	1 cup crumbs
graham crackers	14 squares	1 cup crumbs
saltine crackers	28 crackers	1 cup crumbs
vanilla wafers	22 wafers	1 cup crumbs
Dates, pitted	1 pound	3 cups chopped
	8- ounce package	1½ cups chopped
Eggs	4 large	1 cup
whites	8 to 11	1 cup
yolks	12 to 14	1 cup
Flour, all-purpose	1 pound	3½ cups
cake	1 pound	4¾ to 5 cups sifted
whole-wheat	1 pound	3½ cups unsifted
Green bell pepper	1 large	1 cup diced
Lemon	1 medium	2 to 3 tablespoons juice; 2 teaspoons grated rind
Lettuce	1- pound head	6¼ cups torn
Lime	1 medium	1½ to 2 tablespoons juice; 1½ teaspoons grated rind
Macaroni	4 ounces dry (1 cup)	2 cups cooked
Margarine	1 pound	2 cups
	¼- pound stick	½ cup
Marshmallows	10 large	1 cup
	10 miniature	1 large marshmallow
	½ pound miniature	4½ cups
Milk, evaporated, skim	12- ounce can	1½ cups

FOOD	WEIGHT (OR COUNT)	YIELD
Milk, continued		
sweetened, condensed, fat-free		
or low-fat	14- ounce can	1¼ cups
Mushrooms	3 cups raw (8 ounces)	1 cup sliced cooked
Nuts, almonds	1 pound	1 to 1¾ cups nutmeats
	1 pound shelled	3½ cups nutmeats
peanuts	1 pound	2¼ cups nutmeats
	1 pound shelled	3 cups
pecans	1 pound	2¼ cups nutmeats
	1 pound shelled	4 cups
walnuts	1 pound	1⅔ cups nutmeats
	1 pound shelled	4 cups
Oats, quick-cooking	1 cup	1¾ cups cooked
Onion	1 medium	½ cup chopped
Orange	1 medium	½ cup juice; 2 tablespoons grated rind
Peaches	2 medium	1 cup sliced
Pears	2 medium	1 cup sliced
Potatoes, baking	3 medium	2 cups cubed cooked or 1¾ cups mashed
sweet	3 medium	3 cups sliced
Raisins	1 pound	3 cups
Rice, long-grain	1 cup	3 to 4 cups cooked
quick-cooking	1 cup	2 cups cooked
Shrimp, raw in shell	1½ pounds	2 cups (¾ pound) cleaned, cooked
Spaghetti	7 ounces	About 4 cups cooked
Strawberries	1 quart	4 cups sliced
Sugar, brown	1 pound	2⅓ cups firmly packed
powdered	1 pound	3½ cups unsifted
granulated	1 pound	2 cups

EQUIVALENT MEASURES

3	teaspoons	1	tablespoon
4	tablespoons	¼	cup
5⅓	tablespoons	⅓	cup
8	tablespoons	½	cup
16	tablespoons	1	cup
2	tablespoons (liquid)	1	ounce
1	cup..................................	8	fluid ounces

2	cups.....................	1	pint (16 fluid ounces)
4	cups.....................	1	quart
4	quarts	1	gallon
⅛	cup	2	tablespoons
⅓	cup	5	tablespoons plus 1 teaspoon
⅔	cup	10	tablespoons plus 2 teaspoons
¾	cup	12	tablespoons

allspice A pea-size berry from the pimiento tree, named because it tastes like a combination of cloves, cinnamon, and nutmeg. Purchased as whole berries or ground, it is used in both savory and sweet dishes.

anchovy paste A combination of ground anchovy fillets, vinegar, spices, and water that is packaged in tubes.

balsamic vinegar An Italian vinegar made from white Trebbiano grapes. Aged over a period of years in wooden barrels, the vinegar has a dark color and pungent sweetness.

bread flour A 99.8% hard-wheat unbleached flour with a high gluten content that provides elasticity, which helps yeast breads rise.

cilantro The fresh leaves from the coriander plant. Widely used in Asian and Latin American cooking, it has a pungent flavor that lends itself to spicy foods.

Cointreau A liqueur from France that is clear, colorless, and orange flavored.

cooking apples Apples that remain firm and flavorful when cooked, such as Baldwin, Cortland, Granny Smith, Northern Spy, Rome Beauty, Winesap, and York Imperial.

couscous A staple of North African dining made from semolina, a coarsely ground durum wheat. It takes just 5 minutes to prepare and can be used much like rice.

curly endive A slightly bitter green with prickly leaves that is sometimes mistakenly called chicory.

currants Dried seedless Zante grapes, resembling tiny raisins.

curry powder A traditional Indian blend of up to 20 herbs, spices, and seeds. It is available in two degrees of spiciness: standard and hot (Madras).

Feta cheese A classic white and crumbly Greek cheese with a rich, tangy flavor. Traditionally made with sheep's or goat's milk.

ginger A common spice known for its peppery and sweet flavor. Ginger comes in several forms: fresh (the gnarled root), dried ground, crystallized, and pickled.

julienne To cut into thin matchlike strips, especially vegetables.

kiwifruit An oblong fruit that has a rough brown covering on the outside and bright-green flesh flecked with tiny edible black seeds inside. Eaten peeled, the fruit tastes similar to pineapple and strawberry.

leek Similar in appearance to a giant scallion with a cylindrical white bulb and dark-green leaves. The flavor is like those of garlic and onion but milder and more subtle.

mango A golden-fleshed, juicy, and exotically sweet fruit. The flesh must be carefully carved away from the huge flat seed that traverses the length of the fruit.

molasses The brownish-black syrup produced during the refining of sugar cane and sugar beets.

Neufchâtel cheese A soft, white, unripened cheese similar to cream cheese.

ramekin A baking dish, usually made of porcelain or earthenware, that resembles a miniature soufflé dish.

saffron The world's most expensive spice, made from the yellow-orange stigma of a small purple crocus. Each stigma must be carefully hand-picked and dried. Luckily, saffron is very flavorful, so a little goes a long way.

self-rising flour A blend of all-purpose flour, baking powder, and salt.

shallot A plant related to the onion but formed with a divided bulb like garlic. The shallot has a mild onion flavor.

shiitake mushroom A mushroom with a full-bodied, meaty flavor. The tough stem should be removed.

turmeric The root of a tropical plant related to ginger. It has a bitter, pungent flavor and a bright yellow-orange color.

watercress A plant that grows in cool, running streams and whose pungent, peppery-tasting leaves are often used in salads and soups and as a garnish. Part of the mustard family.

wheat germ The embryo of the wheat kernel that has a nutty flavor. Sold in both toasted and natural forms, wheat germ is a concentrated source of vitamins, minerals, and protein.

wild rice Not really a rice at all, but the grain from a marsh grass native to the northern Great Lakes area. Has a nutty flavor and chewy texture.

Nutrition and Serving-Size Information

Here are some specific guidelines that *Weight Watchers* Magazine adheres to regarding our recipes. For nutritional accuracy, please be sure to follow our suggestions.

• When preparing a recipe that yields more than one serving, it is important to mix the ingredients well and then divide the mixture evenly.

• Where liquid and solid parts have to be divided evenly, drain the liquid and set it aside. Evenly divide the remaining ingredients; then add equal amounts of the liquid to each serving.

• Unless otherwise indicated, servings of meat, poultry, and fish refer to cooked, skinned, and boned servings.

• Recipes provide approximate nutritional information, including the following: CAL (calories), PRO (protein), FAT (total fat), sat (saturated fat), CARB (carbohydrates), FIB (dietary fiber), CHOL (cholesterol), IRON (iron), SOD (sodium), and CALC (calcium). Measurements are abbreviated as follows: g (grams), mg (milligrams).

• Recipes include *POINTS*™ based on Weight Watchers International's 1•2•3 Success™ Weight Loss Plan.

• *POINTS* are calculated from a formula based on calories, fat, and fiber that assigns higher points to higher-calorie, higher-fat foods. Based on your present weight, you are allowed a certain amount of *POINTS* per day.

Note: Because data on fat distribution are not available for some processed foods, these breakdowns should be considered approximate.

• Recipes now include diabetic exchanges, which have been calculated from the *Exchange List for Meal Planning* developed by The American Dietetic Association and the American Diabetes Association. The exchange information is designated as follows: starch, fruit, skim milk (sk milk), low-fat milk (l-f milk), whole milk (wh milk), vegetable (veg), very lean meat, lean meat, medium-fat meat (med-fat meat), high-fat meat (hi-fat meat), and fat.

Each category from the exchange list consists of foods that are similar in their nutritional makeup. Therefore, foods within the same category can be substituted. For example, ½ cup cereal for one slice of bread.

• The recipes that are shown in our photographs may vary as to the number of servings pictured. It is important that you refer to the recipes for the exact serving information.

U S E F U L   E Q U I V A L E N T S   F O R   T E M P E R A T U R E   S E T T I N G S

	Fahrenheit	Celsius	Gas Mark
Freeze Water	32° F	0°C	
Room Temperature	68° F	20° C	
Boil Water	212° F	100° C	
Bake	325° F	160° C	3
	350° F	180° C	4
	375° F	190° C	5
	400° F	200° C	6
	425° F	220° C	7
	450° F	230° C	8
Broil			Grill